# Mizuna

FRENCH-INSPIRED CONTEMPORARY AMERICAN CUISINE

FRANK BONANNO AND JILL ZEH RICHTER

PUBLISHED BY MIZUNA, LLC

MIZUNA
French-Inspired Contemporary American Cuisine
Frank Bonanno and Jill Zeh Richter

Photographed by Bill Cooley (www.cooleyimages.com)

Paintings by Quang Ho

Food styled by Jill Zeh Richter

Designed by Studio Signorella (www.studiosignorella.com)

Edited by Janis Judd

Mizuna
225 East Seventh Avenue
Denver, Colorado 80203

www.mizunadenver.com


Printed in China

Mizuna

Dedication

The restuarant

The Chef

The Frontman

The Staff

Acknowledgements

The Artist

*The Menu*

FOR THE BONANNO SONS LUCA AND MARCO,

MAY THEY SOMEDAY ENJOY FOIE GRAS.

A HEAVILY BEARDED MAN leans over the railing of Mizuna's patio, talking to chef/owner Frank Bonanno. Bonanno wears a fine layer of flour from baking the morning's bread; in his right fist he clutches roughly five pounds of morel mushrooms (a freak fire in the foothills brought out a record crop). The guy with the beard wants to know how many rabbits he will need for the weekend?

All around these two, the Tuesday morning delivery trucks moan into Governer's Park— here's the name of a familiar beer, there's the title of a major food corporation, over there a giant linen company. These trucks block traffic and announce that this is one of Denver's busiest restaurant neighborhoods—but they rattle right past the conversation at the corner of Seventh and Grant. The trucks that loll into the alley behind Mizuna are different, old and small. They bear names like *Red Tomato* and *Intrigue. House of Smoke.*

Bonanno and partner, Doug Fleischmann, opened Mizuna in 2001. Within months the intimate eatery had been lauded by press and locals alike. Mirrored walls, soft lighting, and a small, well run dining room provide a perfect showcase for Bonanno's food—also simple, elegant, and unique. Bonanno's intent was to infuse Denver with styles and techniques he'd picked up working at some of the finest restaurants both in this country and abroad, but that concept quickly evolved into something far more dramatic, something executive chef Alex Seidel describes as "one of the biggest food laboratories in Colorado."

Here chefs are given wide creative berth. Every member of Bonanno's team has input on a menu that changes monthly. Each chef is empowered to order whatever ingredients seem best suited to his station, and the result is an inspiring marriage between science and epicuria. Knives tap quietly and efficiently; white jacketed chefs test rethought versions of old recipes, try out new food combinations and pick through ingredients to find the freshest, sweetest or most savory elements. They discuss topics like the New York Times food section and the quality of American grown truffles. What Frank Bonanno has done at Mizuna is to create an environment where skilled cooks are encouraged to stretch the limits of their palates and broaden their understanding of ingredients both local and exotic. Bonanno's own gifted palate and technique become mentoring tools in his kitchen, and the result is consistently remarkable food, simply prepared, and professionally served. Tiny Mizuna has earned a reputation as a special place among food lovers, but it is more. It is an artist's studio, a culinary think tank, a food laboratory. Mizuna's the place where the rabbit farmer comes to sell his wares.

FRANK BONANNO FOUND HIS passion early, working in restaurants most of his life. After he graduated from the School of Finance at the University of Denver, Bonanno revisited that passion by earning a second degree at the Culinary Institute in Hyde Park, NY. "I had a great childhood, says Bonanno. Most of who I am today comes from the food I was fortunate enough to be exposed to at a very young age." The aroma of pastries and pastas from his Sicilian grandmother permeated Bonanno's New Jersey home where he and his mother tried out old Julia Child's recipes on the family. On weekends his parents would take him to explore the gastronomic wonders of New York City. Bonanno's award-winning restaurants—Mizuna and Luca d'Italia—reflect that upbringing.

Bonanno opened Mizuna after four years at Mel's Bar and Grill, where owner Mel Masters afforded Bonanno opportunity to work at some of the finest eateries in Italy, California, and New York. Bonanno's appreciation for fresh, locally grown items at the peak of their flavor came from a stretch at The French Laundry in California. His ability to prepare those ingredients with speed and finesse was honed at New York eatery Gramercy Tavern. Bonanno "is inspired by classic French techniques, but also by the simplicity of the type of food found in the best American restaurants. I like to offer clean flavors that enhance the freshest, finest ingredients."

While Bonanno believes that the "star" at his restaurants is the food, there is a final feature that makes the dining experiences exemplary. The teams. "Food is a way to express your-self and make people happy. Everyone here is in this business because we love it. That's why we do it. We know were going to serve seventy people dinner tonight, and the best way to do that," he says smiling, "is with passion."

THERE'S AN APHORISM TACKED to Mizuna's office wall, "People don't remember what you say, they remember how you make them feel."

Doug put that there.

Doug Fleischmann, co-founder of Mizuna, once brushed off the idea that he was the reason for the restaurant's acclaim and diner allegiance. "Frank's the star here," Fleischmann said of his partner. But the truth is Mizuna is the house that Doug built. The interior is his design, his art hangs in the dining room; the highly polished waitstaff is the product of his diligent training, and it was his management that brought to Mizuna the elegance and flair that made—makes—Denver diners rave.

Doug's background—from Café Giovanni to the Brown Palace to Strings—made him widely acknowledged as Denver's best frontman. He and Frank hooked up while working a stint at Mel's Bar and Grill, and it was just a short time before the two were making local history. "We walk a fine line," Doug once told a journalist, "giving people a spectacular meal and experience, but in a homespun sort of way. I want people to feel comfortable here." So it was that Doug's gentle laughter set the tone at Mizuna in the early days, and his presence lingers in the beauty of his paintings and in the atmosphere he created.

Doug Fleischmann is the unlisted ingredient in every recipe in this cookbook. Partner, friend, brother—namesake of the youngest Bonanno—we remember how he made us feel, and we only hope for the grace to pass that feeling on.

ALEX SEIDEL notes the connection between cooking and golf: "It's important to remain focused," he says, "and improve a little bit every day." Seidel graduated from the Western Culinary Institute in Portland, and came to be the chef d' cuisine at Mizuna after working in Carmel, Racine, Milwaukee, and ultimately Vail's famed Sweet Basil. "Frank has never set any limits on the experimentation with food or denied me access to the best possible ingredients from all over the world", Seidel notes. His zeal is such that it extends into every arena of his life; for example, he is a cultured gardener whose produce often appears on Mizuna's summer menu. What were the gifts for guests at Seidels recent June wedding? Heirloom tomato seeds.

ANDREW INMAN believes that it's important to "be creative in every area of your life," and he expresses that creativity working the saucier station at Mizuna. Inman, a North Carolina native, has developed strong roots in the Colorado area, working at the reputed Splendito in Beaver Creek, as well as some of the finest venues in Boulder and Denver. When he worked at Borolo Grill, Inman had the opportunity to extensively tour the Toscana and Piemonte regions of Italy, where he discovered a talent for pairing food and wines. "Every smell, every flavor, every texture works together when you are dining. It's my job to find combinations to bring the best flavors, textures, and aromas into harmony."

JEAN PHILIPPE FAILYAU "enjoys keeping up with food trends by reading as much as possible." Failyau runs the grill station at Mizuna and brings a unique multi-national background to the kitchen. The Belgium native arrived in New York after attending the University of Guadalajara, and in 2000 graduated from the French Culinary Institute. After a turn at San Francisco's famed Aqua restaurant, Failyau moved to Colorado for the "quality of life" Denver offers. "I love the culinary freedom at Mizuna and the ability it gives me to use the best and freshest ingredients," Failyau says. "Plus, I work with great people."

# ACKNOWLEDGEMENTS

I HAVE A CHARMED LIFE. To those who helped me accomplish this dream: thank you.

Thank you to the teams at Mizuna and Luca d'Italia Every day I get to go to a job I love and work with people who are passionate about food. Elbow to elbow, twelve hours at a shot, chopping and kneading and lifting and creating in 110 degrees stand the likes of Big A, Droopy and Tony, Billy, Peshek, Stevie and Angela. They are the finest chefs I know, and supported by the best waitstaff in Colorado: Chris, Geoff, Kara and Kathy. Noel and Jimmy. How lucky I am to know such unbelievable talent.

Thank you to my family. First and foremost my increasing love and gratitude to Jacqueline, Marco and Luca– my wife and partner in the restaurants supports every aspect of my crazy life and my sons make me laugh no matter how tired I am. My amazing mother cooked with me and introduced me to Julia Childs; she showed me how to shop for quality food, fresh herbs and produce. Through my father I learned to catch and clean fish. He taught me to respect the ocean and later forgave me for trading up a finance degree for culinary school. He is a rock of support and guidance. My sister Kate is a remarkable cook and baker whose skills and passion continue to influence me. My brothers Chris, Neil, and Tee have always offered encouragement and sound business advice. I even have great in-laws, especially Bea & Jack Drake who traverse eighteen hundred miles and risky culinary territory on our behalf.

Thank you to the great teachers– A special toast to Mel Masters who nurtured my skills as a chef while teaching me the business side of the restaurants ("food cost, baby"). Mel took me into his family and gave me my first real glimpse of epicurea. Another toast to Thomas Keller: although I only worked at the French Laundry for a short period, it was by far the greatest culinary experience of my life. Chef Keller elevates the industry with quality and simplicity.

There is a final appreciation, the level of which is difficult for me to express, that goes to you who would buy this cookbook. The Consummate Diner. You are the food lover who consistently trusts our choices. Without you I would be nothing. So thank you deeply and sincerely Consummate Diners, more of you than I can possibly name, but a few of whom especially come to mind: Mary Lou and Randy Barnhardt, Marty and Sandy Slebodnik, Jeff and Dawn Castardi, Skip and Susanne Norstrand, The Steinbreucks, The Osters, The Schraas, The Trammels, and all the Smiths, Jones and Browns whose palates are rewarded with great food in small restaurants all over the world.

Cheers,
Frank Bonanno

QUANG HO, AN INTERNATIONALLY ACCLAIMED artist, is widely recognized by collectors, galleries, artists and students. Quang's paintings are highly sought after by collectors evidenced by the numerous sold-out shows he has held. Some of the notable collectors include the Prince of Brunai and screen writer Robert Town. His works have won many awards including: The Artists Choice Awards (the highest of honors) from The Artists Of America Exhibition; The North West Rendezvous Show; The Colorado Governor's Show; and The Oil Painters of America Show.

Quang Ho was born in 1963, in Hue, Vietnam. He immigrated to the United States in 1975 and is now a U.S. Citizen. His artistic interest began at the early age of three and continued through grade school, high school, art school and led him to a very exciting and successful painting profession. In 1980, at the age of 16, Quang held his first one-man-show at Tomorrows Masters Gallery in Denver Colorado. The exhibit was a smashing success for the high school sophomore. In 1982, Quang's mother was killed in a tragic auto accident, leaving him the responsibility of raising four younger brothers and a six year old sister. That same year, Quang attended the Colorado Institute of Art on a National Scholastics Art Awards Scholarship. Ho graduated from CIA in 1985 with Best Portfolio Award for the graduating class. Working mostly in oils and occasionally watercolor and pastels, Ho's subject matter ranges from still-life, landscapes, interiors, and dancers, to figuratives. "I can find visual excitement all around me as well as on the canvas– from a knot on a tree, graceful limp of a flower wilting, to a juxtaposition of a few simple shapes and colors... inspirations are inexhaustible."

## First Courses

**BRAISED BABY ARTICHOKES**
*Olives, Roasted Red Peppers, Capers and Roasted Garlic Aïoli*

**WHITE ASPARAGUS**
*Roasted Chanterelles, Pine Nuts, Brie de Meaux*

**BEEF CARPACCIO BENEDICT STYLE**
*Homemade English Muffins*

**DUNGENESS CRAB AND LOBSTER RAVIOLI**
*Marinated Hearts of Palm, Tarragon Buerre Blanc*

**SEARED HUDSON VALLEY FOIE GRAS**
*French Toast Gratin, Fig Jam, Duck Maple Syrup*

**LOBSTER CARPACCIO**
*Yellow Pear and Red Cherry Tomato Salad, Spicy Garlic Aïoli*

**LOBSTER PROFITEROLES**
*Wild Mushroom Duxelle*

**POTATO WRAPPED OYSTERS ROCKEFELLER STYLE**
*Wilted Spinach, Buerre Blanc, Osetra Caviar*

**ASIAN BBQ PORK**
*Shrimp Noodles, Lemon Grass Broth, Scallion Salad*

**BRAISED RABBIT**
*Risotto, Wild Mushroom Ragu, Crispy Shallots*

**SMOKED SALMON**
*Potato-Chive Blini, Crème Fraîche*

**ALMOND CRUSTED SOFTSHELL CRAB**
*Cucumber Gazpacho, Watermelon Radish*

**TUNA SLICED AND DICED**
*Summer Squash Salad, Yuzu Vinaigrette*

**VEAL SWEETBREADS SALTIMBOCCA**
*Spinach Orzo Salad, Sage-Veal Reduction*

# BRAISED BABY ARTICHOKES
*Olives, Roasted Red Peppers, Capers, Roasted Garlic Aïoli*
Serves 4

## BRAISED ARTICHOKES

> 12 baby artichokes
>
> 1 tablespoon fresh lemon juice
>
> 1 tablespoon plus ¼ cup extra virgin olive oil
>
> 1 leek, julienned
>
> ¼ cup white wine
>
> 1 cup water

Trim off the stem end of each artichoke so it is even with the bottom, then cut off the top half of each artichoke. Cut the artichokes into quarters and place them in acidulated water until ready to poach. (That is water with a little lemon juice, so that the edges don't turn brown.)

Place 1 tablespoon of the olive oil in a medium sauce pan over high heat. Add the leeks and sauté them until softened, 3–4 minutes; do not let color. You may have to reduce the heat slightly. When the leeks have softened, drain the water from the artichokes and add them to the sauce pan. Deglaze with the white wine, letting it reduce until the pan is dry. Add the water, cover the pan, bring to a boil, reduce to low and simmer covered 20 minutes or until the artichokes are tender. To check tenderness, poke a fork in the center of the artichoke. If it is tender, they are done. Remove the artichokes from the water, and toss with remaining ¼ cup olive oil. Chill.

## GARNISHES

> 20-24 olives
>
> 4 tablespoons large capers
>
> 2 red peppers, roasted, peeled, seeded and sliced (see recipe page 167)
>
> 1 cup roasted garlic aïoli (see recipe page 161)
>
> basil oil (see recipe page 163)
>
> Parmesan cheese

TO SERVE. Place the artichokes, olives, capers and peppers in a large sauté pan over medium heat. Cook until the ingredients are warm. Divide the artichokes, olives, capers and peppers among 4 appetizer plates. Place the aïoli in a small squeeze tube and drizzle over the plate. Then drizzle with basil oil and shave Parmesan cheese on top.

## WHITE ASPARAGUS
*Roasted Chanterelles, Pine Nuts, Brie de Meaux*
Serves 6

This is a great way to start a meal in the fall.

2 bunches white asparagus, peeled and ends trimmed

2 cups fresh chanterelles (if you can't find them, substitute shiitakes)

2 tablespoons olive oil

2 tablespoons minced fresh thyme

salt and white pepper

8 ounces pine nuts

1/2 pound Brie de Meaux, cut into 6 small wedges

2 bunches fresh watercress

1 teaspoon fresh lemon juice

2 tablespoons olive oil

Preheat the oven to 400°F. Bring a large pot of water to a boil. Add the asparagus 1/2 bunch at a time, and blanch for 3–5 minutes until tender. Shock the asparagus in ice water to stop the cooking process.

Toss the chanterelles in a bowl with the olive oil, thyme, salt and pepper. Place the chanterelles on a baking sheet and put in the oven. Roast the mushrooms until they are golden, about 20 minutes. Remove them from the oven and reduce the heat to 200°F.

Place the pine nuts in a small sauté pan over low heat. Toast the nuts until they start to turn brown. Check and stir often as they can burn easily!

Place the asparagus and Brie slices on the baking sheet with the mushrooms and place back in the oven. Roast until the asparagus is warm and the Brie begins to melt.

TO SERVE. Toss the watercress with the lemon juice and olive oil. Divide the mixture among 6 salad plates. Remove the baking sheet from the oven and place 1 slice of Brie, a few mushrooms and several asparagus spears on each plate. Top with the pine nuts.

# BEEF CARPACCIO BENEDICT STYLE
*Homemade English Muffins*

Serves 6

This is a new twist on an old favorite. Be sure to ask for the tail end of the beef tenderloin.

## HOLLANDAISE SAUCE

| | |
|---|---|
| 2 sticks butter | 1 teaspoon lemon juice |
| 2 egg yolks | salt and white pepper |

Melt the butter in a small saucepan. Skim the foam from the top and let the milk solids sink to the bottom of the pan. Carefully pour the clarified butter into a liquid measuring cup.

Fill a saucepan with water and bring to a simmer. Place the egg yolks and lemon juice in a small bowl that will just fit inside the saucepan. Whisk the egg yolk mixture over the pan of simmering water until the eggs have thickened and are pale yellow in color. (You may need a folded kitchen towel between the bowl and the pan to keep the bowl steady.) Incorporate the butter by adding it slowly in a thin stream while continuously whisking the yolks. Season the hollandaise with salt and pepper to taste. Keep warm.

## BEEF TENDERLOIN

| | |
|---|---|
| 6 ounces beef tenderloin | Extra virgin olive oil |

Slice the tenderloin on the bias, $\frac{1}{4}$ inch thick. You should have 3–4 slices per person. Lightly oil the beef with olive oil and lay the slices out flat on the work surface. Cover the slices with plastic wrap and pound with a meat mallet to flatten.

## POACHED EGGS

| | |
|---|---|
| 6 large eggs | 2 tablespoons white wine vinegar |

Bring a large pot of water to boil. Add the vinegar and reduce the heat to simmer. Gently drop the eggs into the pot and poach for 3–4 minutes, until the whites are set. Carefully remove the eggs from the water with a slotted spoon. Absorb any excess moisture with a towel. Keep warm. Season with salt and white pepper.

## TO SERVE.

| | |
|---|---|
| 3 whole wheat English muffins (see recipe page166) | Black truffle shavings |
| butter | Chervil |
| 1 bunch watercress | Truffle oil |

Toast and then butter the English muffin halves. Place one in the center of 6 appetizer plates. Arrange a circle of fanned out watercress around the muffins and fan out the sliced beef on top of the muffins. Place a poached egg on top of the beef and top that with some Hollandaise, truffle and chervil. Drizzle with truffle oil.

# DUNGENESS CRAB AND LOBSTER RAVIOLI
*Marinated Hearts of Palm, Tarragon Buerre Blanc*
Serves 8

It is important that you have a female lobster, because you need the coral (raw roe sack) to make the pasta. If you are squeamish about cutting a live lobster, you may want to have them cut it apart where you buy it.

## LOBSTER MEAT

$1\frac{1}{4}$ pound live female lobster, separate out the roe sack (read below)

Place the lobster on a cutting board. (Put a towel under your cutting board so it doesn't slip.) Hold the lobster steady with your left hand. With a French knife in your right hand quickly jab the tip into the center of the lobster's head and push the knife through until it hits the cutting board. Then bring the knife down horizontally through the eyes and split the head in half. That will kill the lobster instantly. Twist off the tail and the claws and reserve. Then cut the lobster body in half and remove the green roe sack (coral).

Place the claws and tail in separate bowls. Bring a large pot of water to a boil and pour the boiling water over claws and tail. Make sure they are completely submerged. Let the claws steep for 6 minutes and the tail for 4 minutes. Remove all the lobster meat from the hot water and immediately place it in ice water to stop the cooking process. When cool, remove the meat from the shells.

## CORAL PASTA DOUGH

The dough will be green until you cook it and then it will turn pink. You will have extra dough, lay extra squares in an even layer on a baking sheet and place in the freezer. When frozen transfer to an airtight container until ready to use.

8 egg yolks

1 raw lobster roe sack (coral)

2 cups flour

1 cup semolina

1 tablespoon salt

2 tablespoons olive oil

$\frac{1}{2} - \frac{3}{4}$ cup water

Place the egg yolks and the lobster roe in the bowl of a food processor. Pulse to combine. Then add the flour, semolina and salt. Pulse a few times until the ingredients are incorporated. Add the olive oil and $\frac{1}{2}$ cup water. Pulse a few more times until the dough comes together. If the dough appears crumbly, add more water, 1 tablespoon at a time, until it appears smooth and elastic. Wrap the dough in plastic wrap, place in the refrigerator. Let it rest 1 hour. Remove the dough from the refrigerator and let it warm to room temperature. Set the pasta machine on the widest setting. Flatten the dough into a rectangle. The short side should be the same width as the pasta machine. Roll the dough through. Turn the machine to the next setting and roll the dough through again. Try to keep the dough in an even rectangle. Continue to move to a thinner setting, one notch at a time until the dough is $\frac{1}{16}$ inch thick. If the pasta sheets get to long to manage, cut them in half. Cut the pasta sheets into 4 inch squares with a fluted pastry wheel. You can make this part ahead of time and freeze the squares until you are ready to use them. When you are ready to serve, bring a large pot of salted water to a boil. Drop 16 of the squares of pasta into the water and cook 2–3 minutes until they turn pink. (You may need to do this in two batches.) Remove the pasta gently from the water with a spider and lay the pasta squares in one layer on lightly oiled baking sheets until ready to use.

### MARINATED HEARTS OF PALM

> 1 tablespoon olive oil
>
> $\frac{1}{4}$ cup finely diced red onion
>
> $\frac{1}{4}$ cup finely diced celery
>
> 3 tablespoon butter
>
> 1 cup finely diced hearts of palm
>
> 8 ounces Dungeness crabmeat
>
> reserved lobster tail and claw meat, coarsely chopped
>
> 2 tablespoons fresh Meyer lemon juice
>
> 4 tablespoons extra virgin olive oil
>
> salt and white pepper

Place the olive oil in a small sauté pan over medium-high heat. Add the onion and celery and sweat until tender. Add the butter. When the butter has melted, add the hearts of palm, crabmeat, lobster, lemon juice and olive oil. Heat through and then season to taste with salt and pepper.

### TARRAGON BUERRE BLANC

> buerre blanc (see recipe page 162)
>
> tarragon oil (see recipe page 163)
>
> microgreens

Make the buerre blanc and then fold in 2–4 tablespoons of the tarragon oil.

TO SERVE. Place one pasta square in the center of each plate. Place 2–3 tablespoons of the hearts of palm salad on top of each square. Then top that with another pasta square, making the corners opposite one another. Drizzle the tarragon beurre blanc over the ravioli and around the plate. Top the ravioli with microgreens, then drizzle the plate with tarragon oil.

# SEARED HUDSON VALLEY FOIE GRAS
*French Toast Gratin, Fig Jam, Duck Maple Syrup*
Serves 4

Hudson Valley Foie Gras is an award winning domestic product. You can buy it online at hudsonvalleyfoiegras.com

## FIG JAM

> 1 tablespoon olive oil
>
> 2 shallots, minced
>
> 9 ounces dried figs, quartered, stems removed
>
> 1 tablespoon brown sugar
>
> 1 cup port
>
> salt and white pepper

Heat the olive oil in a small saucepan. Add the shallots and sweat until translucent. Add the figs and brown sugar, then deglaze with the port. Bring the mixture to a boil, reduce the heat to a simmer, cover and let it cook until the liquid has been absorbed. Cool to room temperature. Pulse the figs in a food processor. It may be necessary to add a couple of tablespoons of water to create a smooth jam-like consistency. Season to taste with salt and pepper.

## DUCK MAPLE SYRUP

> $^3/_4$ cup duck stock (see recipe page 159)
>
> $^1/_4$ cup maple syrup

Bring the duck stock to a boil in a small saucepan. Boil until the stock is reduced by half, then add the maple syrup. Bring the mixture back to a boil, then remove from the heat.

## FRENCH TOAST

> $^1/_4$ loaf brioche (see recipe page 165)
>
> 1 egg, beaten
>
> $^1/_2$ cup heavy cream
>
> dash cinnamon
>
> 3 tablespoons clarified butter (see recipe page 162)

Cut 4 slabs ($^1/_2$ inch thick) of brioche. Using a 3 inch diameter ring mold, cut a circle out of the middle of each slice of the brioche. Place the circles in one layer on a baking sheet and set out over night to dry the bread.

Mix the egg, cream and cinnamon together in a small bowl. Heat the clarified butter in a sauté pan. Dip the bread slices into the egg mixture and place in the pan. Cook 3 minutes per side until golden brown.

### FOIE GRAS

> 4 slices of foie gras (3 ounces each)
>
> salt and white pepper
>
> chervil

Season the foie gras liberally with salt and white pepper. Place a small sauté pan over high heat. When hot, add the foie gras and sear 1 minute per side.

TO SERVE. Place one slice of French toast in the center of each plate. Top with 1 tablespoon fig jam and 1 slice of seared foie gras. Garnish with chervil, drizzle the plate with duck maple syrup.

# LOBSTER CARPACCIO
## *Yellow Pear and Red Cherry Tomato Confit, Spicy Garlic Aïoli*
Serves 4

The term Carpaccio is Italian in origin and usually consists of thin shavings of raw beef fillet that have been drizzled with olive oil and lemon juice. In this recipe, we gently poach the lobster tails, slice them as thinly as possible and toss them with olive oil and lemon juice.

### TO POACH THE LOBSTER

2 raw lobster tails, 5–6 ounces each

1 small onion, diced

2 ribs celery, diced

1 carrot, peeled and diced

1 lemon, halved

3 sprigs parsley

$\frac{1}{4}$ cup olive oil

1 tablespoon fresh lemon juice

salt and white pepper

To keep the lobster tails from curling while they are being poached you will need to place a metal skewer through the center of each tail. Start at the meaty end of the tail and push the skewer through the center. Keep pushing until the skewer goes through the fan end of the tail. Place the onion, celery, carrot, lemon and parsley in a pot large enough to hold the lobster tails without crowding. Fill the pot with water, bring to a boil and add the lobster tails. Then turn off the heat and let sit for 6 minutes. Remove the tails from the water and place them in ice water to chill. Remove the tails from the ice water, and gently remove the meat from the shell by cutting up the underside of the tail with kitchen shears. Slice the lobster meat into $\frac{1}{4}$ inch thick pieces, drizzle with olive oil and lemon juice, season with salt and pepper. Place in the refrigerator to marinate.

## Yellow Pear and Red Cherry Tomato Confit

    1 cup yellow pear tomatoes, halved

    1 cup red cherry tomatoes, halved

    ¼ cup finely diced red onion

    1 tablespoon capers

    ¼ cup chiffonade basil leaves

    1 teaspoon balsamic vinegar

    1 cup olive oil

    salt and white pepper

Mix the pear tomatoes, cherry tomatoes, onion, capers, basil and vinegar together in a bowl. Place the olive oil in a small pan and warm to 160°F. Pour the oil into the tomato mixture and stir to coat evenly. Let cool to room temperature. Season to taste with salt and pepper.

## Spicy Garlic Aïoli

    basic aïoli (see recipe page 161)

    1 teaspoon cayenne, or to taste

Mix the cayenne into the aïoli; chill and let rest 30 minutes.

## Garnishes

    chervil

    basil oil (see recipe page 163)

**To serve.** Pack ¼ of the tomato confit into a 3 inch ring mold in the center of each of four appetizer plates then gently remove the ring mold. Divide the lobster slices among the plates and fan out in front of the tomato confit. Top the tomato confit with a dollop of aïoli, (about 1 tablespoon) and top the aïoli with a sprig of chervil. Drizzle the plate with a little basil oil.

# LOBSTER PROFITEROLES
*Wild Mushroom Duxelles*
### Makes about 20 Profiteroles

## PÂTE À CHOUX

$\frac{1}{2}$ cup butter

$\frac{1}{2}$ cup water

$\frac{1}{2}$ cup milk

1 cup flour

$\frac{1}{4}$ teaspoon salt

4 eggs

2 tablespoons duxelles (see recipe below), reserve remainder for filling

Preheat the oven to 375°F. Very lightly grease a baking sheet. Melt the butter in a small sauce pan over medium high heat. Add the water and milk and bring to a simmer. Add the flour and salt and stir with a wooden spoon until the mixture comes together. Continue cooking and stirring 5 minutes more. Take the pan off of the heat and let the mixture cool slightly. Beat in the eggs one at a time. The mixture will break apart, but continue stirring and it will come back together. After the eggs are incorporated, add 1 tablespoon of the duxelle. Place the mixture in a pastry bag fitted with a number 12 tip. Squeeze out puffs about the size of limes. You should have enough choux paste to pipe approximately 20 puffs. They will have small "tips" on top from piping so take a small spatula, dip it in water, and smooth the tips down with the spatula. Place the baking sheet in the oven and bake 20–25 minutes, until the profiteroles are puffed and golden. Let them cool slightly. Split them in half horizontally and place the bases on a serving tray.

## DUXELLES

1 tablespoon olive oil

1 tablespoon minced shallot

2 pounds wild mushrooms, finely diced

1 tablespoon minced thyme

salt and black pepper

Place the olive oil in a sauté pan over medium-high heat. Add the shallots and cook until tender. Add the mushrooms and thyme. Cook until the mushrooms soften and release their liquid. Continue cooking until all the liquid has evaporated. Season the mushrooms with salt and pepper.

## FILLING

    1 tablespoon olive oil

    1 shallot, minced

    reserved duxelles

    2 tablespoons brandy

    1 cup heavy cream

    meat from 1 lobster, chopped, about $2\frac{1}{2}$ cups (see recipe page 7)

    1 cup Parmesan cheese, grated

Place the olive oil in a small sauce pan over medium high heat. Add the shallots and sauté until tender. Add the duxelles and cook until the pan is dry. Deglaze the pan with the brandy, add the cream and reduce the liquid by $\frac{1}{3}$. Add the lobster and heat through. Stir in the Parmesan cheese; season with salt and white pepper.

TO SERVE. Spoon the filling into the profiterole bottoms and then replace the tops. Serve immediately.

# POTATO WRAPPED OYSTERS ROCKEFELLER STYLE
## *Wilted Spinach, Beurre Blanc, Osetra Caviar*
Serves 4

2 large Idaho potatoes

1 teaspoon fresh lemon juice

3 bunches baby spinach, washed and dried, stems removed

16 large oysters

1 cup rock salt

8 ounces beurre blanc (see recipe page 162)

3 tablespoons butter

$\frac{1}{4}$ cup heavy cream

$\frac{1}{4}$ cup Parmesan cheese, grated

salt and white pepper

1 ounce Osetra caviar

Preheat the deep fryer to 400°F. Bring a small pot of water to a boil. Using a mandolin, thinly slice the potatoes lengthwise. Place the potato slices in the boiling water and blanch 60 seconds. Immediately transfer the potatoes into a bowl of ice water mixed with lemon juice. Then blanch the spinach for 30 seconds, drain and shock in ice water.

Shuck the oysters, reserving the meat and shells separately. Refrigerate the oysters until you are ready to use them. Wash and dry 16 oyster shells. Spread the rock salt evenly over the base of a large serving plate. Arrange the oyster shells in the rock salt around the plate.

Make the buerre blanc and keep it warm.

Melt the butter in a sauté pan over high heat. Add the cream and reduce it slightly. Fold in the spinach and Parmesan cheese, and season with salt and pepper. Distribute the spinach evenly in each oyster shell.

Wrap a potato slice around each reserved oyster and secure with a toothpick.

Place half the potato-wrapped oysters in a fry basket and submerge in the hot oil. Cook until the potatoes are crispy, about 3-5 minutes. Remove the potato-wrapped oysters from the oil, let drain, season with salt and pepper, then place on top of the spinach in the oyster shell. Fry the remaining oysters.

TO SERVE. Pour 1 tablespoon of the beurre blanc over each oyster. Top with $\frac{1}{4}$ teaspoon of the caviar.

# ASIAN BBQ PORK
*Shrimp Noodles, Lemon Grass Broth, Scallion Salad*
Serves 6

## BRAISED PORK BELLY

>1 tablespoon olive oil
>
>1 pound skinless pork belly (if you can't find pork belly you can use slab bacon,
>    but remove the rind)
>
>salt and white pepper
>
>$\frac{1}{2}$ cup hoisin sauce
>
>1 cup onion, diced
>
>1 cup celery, diced
>
>1 cup carrot, diced
>
>2 tablespoons tomato paste
>
>$\frac{1}{2}$ cup white wine
>
>2 cups water

Heat the olive oil in a pot with a lid, large enough to hold the pork without crowding it. Season the pork with salt and pepper, then sear the pork on all sides. Remove the pork from the pot and brush it with $\frac{1}{2}$ of the hoisin sauce. Add the onion, celery and carrot to the pot and cover. Sweat the vegetables until they are tender. Remove the lid and let the liquid evaporate. Add the tomato paste and cook 3–4 minutes. Stir so that it coats the vegetables and let it caramelize slightly. Place the pork back in the pot and deglaze with white wine. Add enough water to cover the bottom $\frac{1}{3}$ of the pork. Bring to a boil, reduce the heat to low, cover and simmer the pork 3 hours until tender. Remove the pork from the pot, brush again with the other $\frac{1}{2}$ of the hoisin sauce and let rest 20 minutes. Slice $\frac{1}{2}$ inch thick.

## SCALLION SALAD

>3 bunches scallions, thinly sliced on the bias
>
>1 tablespoon rice wine vinegar
>
>1 tablespoon mirin
>
>1 tablespoon sesame oil
>
>2 tablespoons olive oil

Toss all of the ingredients together in a small bowl.

## LEMON GRASS BROTH

2 stalks lemon grass, cut into quarters

Shells from 1 pound shrimp (see Shrimp Noodles recipe, below)

1 carrot, peeled and diced

$\frac{1}{2}$ onion, diced

2 stalks celery, diced

2 tablespoons ginger, minced

3 cloves garlic, minced

1 bay leaf

3 cups water

salt and white pepper

Place all of the ingredients in a small saucepan over high heat. Bring to a boil, then reduce heat to low and simmer for 20 minutes. Strain, return broth to the saucepan, reheat and season with salt and pepper to taste.

## SHRIMP NOODLES

1 pound raw shrimp peeled and deveined (save shells for lemongrass broth)

3 eggs

4 tablespoons cornstarch

2 tablespoons butter

salt and white pepper

Bring a large pot of water to a boil. Place the shrimp in the bowl of a food processor and purée. Add the eggs and pulse to incorporate. Add the cornstarch and pulse again to incorporate. Fill a pastry bag fitted with a number 7 tip with the shrimp mixture. Squeeze out strands into the boiling water to create noodles. (You will have to do several batches.) Cook 2–3 minutes, remove from water with slotted spoon or spider and place into ice water to stop the cooking process. Let water come back to a full rolling boil between batches. When you are ready to serve the noodles, reheat them in a sauté pan with butter and season with salt and pepper.

TO SERVE. Divide the noodles into 6 serving bowls. Top each with 2–3 slices of pork. Ladle the lemongrass broth around noodles and top the pork with some scallion salad.

# BRAISED RABBIT
*Risotto, Wild Mushroom Ragu, Crispy Shallots*
Serves 4

## BRAISED RABBIT

    1 tablespoon olive oil

    1 small rabbit (3 pounds), quartered

    salt and white pepper

    1 cup diced onion

    1 cup peeled and diced carrots

    1 cup diced celery

    $\frac{1}{4}$ cup tomato paste

    3 cloves garlic

    1 cup white wine

    3–4 cups water

    1 bouquet garni (see recipe page 168)

Preheat the oven to 350°F. Place the olive oil over high heat in a pot large enough to hold the rabbit without crowding. Season the rabbit with salt and pepper, then place it in the pot. Sear the rabbit approximately 10 minutes per side. Remove the rabbit from the pot and add the onion, carrots, and celery. Sweat until translucent. Add the tomato paste and stir to coat the vegetables. Continue cooking until the tomato paste begins to caramelize. Place the rabbit back in the pot, add the garlic and deglaze with white wine. Be sure to scrape up all the browned bits on the bottom and sides of the pan. Add the water and bouquet garni (the rabbit should be about $\frac{1}{3}$ submerged in liquid), bring to a simmer, cover the pot and place it in the oven. Braise for 2–3 hours, until the rabbit meat is tender and pulls easily from the bone. Remove the rabbit from the pot, let it cool slightly, then remove the meat from the skin and bones. Strain the braising liquid through a chinois into another pot. Cook over medium-high heat until the braising liquid is reduced to 1 cup.

## RISOTTO

    1 tablespoon olive oil

    1 tablespoon minced shallot

    1 tablespoon minced garlic

    1 cup carnarolli rice

    $\frac{1}{4}$ cup white wine

    1 cup warm water

    2 tablespoons butter

    $\frac{1}{2}$ cup grated Parmesan

Place the olive oil in a small saucepan over high heat. Add the shallots, garlic and rice and toast, stirring constantly, 3–4 minutes. Do not let brown. Deglaze with the white wine and stir until the rice absorbs all of the liquid. Reduce the heat and add the water $\frac{1}{4}$ cup at a time, stirring after each addition until all the liquid has been absorbed. When the rice is al dente, (after 18–20 minutes), turn off the heat, and add the butter and parmesan. Stir until incorporated.

### WILD MUSHROOM RAGU

    1 tablespoon olive oil

    1 tablespoon minced shallots

    1 tablespoon minced garlic

    2 cups sliced wild mushrooms

    rabbit meat–reserved

    3 tablespoons butter

    salt and white pepper

Place the olive oil in a medium sauté pan over high heat. Add the shallots and garlic. Sweat 2 minutes, being sure not to let them caramelize. Add the mushrooms and sauté them until they begin to release liquid. Add the rabbit and heat through. Stir in the butter and season with salt and pepper.

### CRISPY SHALLOTS

    8 shallots, thinly sliced

    1 tablespoon flour

    3 tablespoons olive oil

Toss the shallots in the flour. Place the olive oil in a small sauce pan over high heat. When oil is hot, add the shallots and cook 2–3 minutes until crispy. Remove the shallots from the oil with a slotted spoon or spider. Drain on paper towels.

TO SERVE. Place $\frac{1}{4}$ cup of the risotto in center of each plate using a 3 inch ring mold. Fill it about $\frac{1}{2}$ way up. Press the risotto down gently with the back of a spoon. Fill the remaining half of the mold with the mushroom and rabbit mixture. Again press down lightly with a spoon, then remove the ring mold. Spoon 2–3 tablespoons of the reduced braising liquid around the plate. Top with the shallots.

# SMOKED SALMON
## *Potato-Chive Blini, Crème Frâiche*
Serves 12

You can usually buy an inexpensive smoker at your local camping supply store. For this recipe we used a "Little Chief". You can find them online at www.smoke-house.com.

## SMOKED SALMON

2½ pound side of fresh salmon

½ cup kosher salt

½ cup brown sugar

4 large sprigs fresh dill

4 large sprigs fresh tarragon

Make sure there are no pin bones left in the salmon. Run your hand over the top of the fillet and you can feel them poking out. If there are some left, take a pair of sheep nose (long and thin) pliers and pull them out. Line a jelly roll pan with enough plastic wrap to go around the salmon. Mix the salt and brown sugar together. Place half the mixture under the salmon (skin side down on top of the plastic wrap.) Place the remaining half of brown sugar/salt mixture on top of the salmon. Make sure it is evenly covered. Place the dill and tarragon sprigs on top of the salt/sugar mixture. Wrap the plastic wrap tightly around the salmon and refrigerate for 24–48 hours.

Remove the salmon from the refrigerator. Unwrap the salmon and rinse off any remaining cure. Gently pat it dry. Rinse off the tray, dry it and lay the salmon back on it, skin side down. Place the salmon back in the refrigerator for 24 hours. This will allow the salmon to form a shiny, slightly tacky skin, a pellicle. It forms on the flesh side of the salmon, and keeps the remaining moisture inside the salmon forming a barrier, so that the fish does not absorb too much smoke during the cold smoking process.

Remove the salmon from the refrigerator and place in a cold smoker for 2 hours. Let it cool, then wrap it in plastic wrap and keep refrigerated until ready to use.

Place the salmon on a cutting board, and using a thin, flexible knife, slice very thin pieces off. Start at the tail end and at a 45 degree angle, work your way up the side.

*—this recipe continues on the following page*

## POTATO CHIVE BLINI
Makes about 25 cakes

>1 cup heavy cream
>
>1 teaspoon active dry yeast
>
>¼ cup buckwheat flour
>
>1 cup all-purpose flour
>
>2 eggs, beaten
>
>1 cup riced cooked potato
>
>2 tablespoons minced chives
>
>¼ cup clarified butter (see recipe page 162)

Heat the cream in a small sauce pan over low heat. When barely warm, add the yeast and let the mixture sit for 3 minutes. In a small bowl, stir together the 2 flours. In another small bowl, mix the eggs into the potatoes. Combine all of these mixtures into a large bowl. Fold in the chives. Heat 2–3 tablespoons of clarified butter on a large griddle. Place 2–3 tablespoons of the batter onto the griddle and let cook 2 minutes then flip and cook for 2 minutes more. Keep the blini warm.

## GARNISHES

>4 eggs, hard boiled
>
>3 shallots, finely minced
>
>¾ cup capers
>
>crème fraîche (see recipe page 162)
>
>1 ounce osetra caviar
>
>chives
>
>red onion powder (see recipe page 167)

TO SERVE. Cut the eggs in half and separate them into yolks and whites. Place the yolks in a mesh strainer and press through with the back of a spoon. Repeat with the whites. Place one blini in the center of the plate, fold up a slice of smoked salmon and place it on top, repeat this process. Then place about a tablespoon each of finely minced shallots, strained egg white, capers and strained egg yolk on the side of the plate. Top the salmon with crème fraiche, caviar and chives. Garnish the plate with red onion powder. (see photo previous page)

## Almond Crusted Softshell Crab
### *Cucumber Gazpacho, Watermelon Radish*
Serves 6

Soft shell crabs are available in the spring. You will want to have them cleaned before you buy them.

### Cucumber Gazpacho

The important thing here is to cut all the ingredients the same size. This will be great practice for your knife skills!

> 1 English cucumber
>
> 1 small zucchini
>
> $\frac{1}{2}$ red onion
>
> 1 green jalapeño
>
> 1 red jalapeño
>
> 1 stalk celery
>
> 2 limes, juiced
>
> 1 tablespoon sherry vinegar
>
> 1 tablespoon minced mint
>
> 1 tablespoon olive oil
>
> salt and white pepper

Cut the cucumber and zucchini in half lengthwise and scoop out seeds. Place the seeds in a chinois and press to squeeze out the juice, reserve. Brunoise the cucumber, zucchini, onion, jalapeños and celery. Place the ingredients in a small bowl and add the reserved cucumber and zucchini juice, lime juice, sherry vinegar, mint and olive oil. Season to taste with salt and pepper.

### Watermelon Radish

> 1 tablespoon minced garlic
>
> $\frac{1}{4}$ cup olive oil
>
> 2 tablespoons fresh lemon juice
>
> pinch sugar
>
> salt and white pepper
>
> 2 watermelon radishes, julienned

In a small bowl, whisk together the garlic, olive oil, lemon juice and sugar. Season to taste with salt and pepper. Add the watermelon radish and mix thoroughly.

*—this recipe continues on the following page*

    6 softshell crabs, cleaned

    2 cups buttermilk

    1 cup almonds (see recipe for toasting nuts page 167)

    1 cup flour

    peanut oil

    cilantro oil (see recipe page 164)

    paprika

Soak the crabs in buttermilk for 2 hours. Preheat peanut oil in deep fryer to 350°F. Toast the almonds and then grind them in a food processor. Mix the flour and ground almonds together in a small bowl. Remove the crabs from the buttermilk and place them in the flour mixture. Coat evenly. Fry the crabs for 2 minutes until they are crispy. Drain.

TO SERVE. Spoon the cucumber gazpacho onto the center of 6 appetizer plates. Top with the watermelon radish and softshell crab. Drizzle the plate with cilantro oil and sprinkle with paprika.

# TUNA SLICED AND DICED
*Summer Squash Salad, Yuzu Vinaigrette*
    Serves 10

Make sure you get the best sushi grade tuna available. These cone shaped "cookies" look difficult, but they are really quite simple to make.

## SESAME TUILE

You will need 2 small cone shaped molds to shape the tuiles. You can buy them at most cooking stores.

> 4 tablespoons butter
>
> $\frac{1}{2}$ cup powdered sugar
>
> $\frac{1}{3}$ cup light corn syrup (3 ounces)
>
> $\frac{1}{3}$ cup flour
>
> 1 teaspoon black sesame seeds
>
> 1 teaspoon sesame oil

Place the butter and powdered sugar in the bowl of a standing mixer that is fitted with a paddle attachment. Mix on low speed until well blended. It should look like course ground corn meal. Add the corn syrup and mix until well blended. Repeat with the flour, then the sesame seeds and the oil. Mix until well incorporated. Place the batter in the refrigerator for about 1 hour until it is completely chilled.

Preheat the oven to 375F. Be sure to use a baking sheet that does not warp in the oven. Place 2 teaspoons of the batter onto the baking sheet. The batter will spread into approximately a 4 inch circle, so space the batter accordingly. Bake for about 8 minutes, until the batter has spread to an even layer and has begun to caramelize. The batter should be an even light brown color when you remove it from the oven. Let the tuile cool on the baking sheet until it stops bubbling. Slide a small metal spatula under the tuile to make sure it is not stuck to the pan. Then place the cone mold on the edge of the tuile. Lift the edge of the tuile up over the cone and roll the tuile around the mold. Keep the tuile tight to the cone. Leave the cone inside the rolled tuile until it has cooled enough to keep its shape. Repeat with the remaining batter.

*—this recipe continues on the following page*

31

### TUNA FILLING

$\frac{1}{2}$ pound sushi grade yellowfin tuna, finely diced

1 ripe avocado, finely diced

$\frac{1}{2}$ English cucumber, peeled, seeded and finely diced

$\frac{1}{2}$ jalapeño pepper, seeded and finely diced

1 tablespoon sesame oil

1 tablespoon soy sauce

1 tablespoon minced cilantro

salt and white pepper

Mix all ingredients together in a small bowl and chill.

### SUMMER SQUASH SALAD

1 small yellow squash

1 small zucchini

3 tablespoons minced cilantro

3 tablespoons soy sauce

1 tablespoon sambal

1 tablespoon yuzu juice

2 tablespoons sesame oil

Using a mandoline, julienne the outside of the yellow squash and zucchini, discarding the seeded core. Mix together the cilantro, soy sauce, sambal, yuzu juice and seasame oil and toss with the summer squash, reserving a few tablespoons.

### GARNISHES

$\frac{1}{2}$ pound sushi grade yellowfin tuna, sliced into 10 pieces

cilantro leaves

TO SERVE. Place a little of the squash mixture in the center of each plate. Lay one slice of tuna on the squash, fill the tuile with chopped tuna mixture and lay on top of the squash. Then drizzle a little of the dressing left from the squash onto each plate. Garnish with cilantro leaves. Serve immediately.

# VEAL SWEETBREADS SALTIMBOCCA
*Spinach Orzo Salad, Sage-Veal Reduction*
Serves 4

Saltimbocca translated from Italian, means "jump mouth," because the dish is soooo good it almost jumps into your mouth. Saltimbocca is traditionally made from thin slices of veal, but we have altered it slightly by using sweetbreads. We pressed them into a thin layer, then finish them traditionally with sage, aged prosciutto, butter and white wine.

## SWEETBREADS

1 pound veal sweetbreads

milk

1 small yellow onion, diced

2 ribs celery, diced

2 carrots, diced

2 slices prosciutto

Place the sweetbreads in a small non-reactive container and cover them with milk. Let them soak for 12 hours, then drain the milk from the sweetbreads. Cover the sweetbreads with fresh milk and let them soak another 12 hours. Drain.

Place the onion, celery and carrots in a small pot and cover with water. Bring to a boil, reduce to a simmer, then add the sweetbreads. DO NOT BOIL. Cook for 8 minutes. Drain the sweetbreads and place side by side in an even layer on a baking sheet, between 2 layers of plastic wrap. Top with another baking sheet and place something heavy on top of it to press the sweetbreads into a flat even layer. Leave overnight. Cut the sweetbreads into 4 equal squares. Cut prosciutto slices in half lengthwise and wrap around sweetbread square and refrigerate until ready to serve.

## SAGE-VEAL REDUCTION

2 cups veal stock (see recipe page 158)

2 tablespoons chiffonade sage

Place the stock and sage in a small sauce pot. Bring to a simmer and reduce the liquid by half. Keep warm until ready to serve.

*—this recipe continues on the following page*

## Spinach Orzo Salad

    3 tablespoons olive oil

    4 sage leaves

    2 tablespoons diced shallots

    2 cups cooked orzo

    1 bunch spinach, stems removed, blanched and chopped

    2 tablespoons butter

    salt and white pepper

Heat 2 tablespoons of the olive oil in a small sauté pan over high heat. Place the sage leaves in the oil and fry until crisp, about 1 minute. Remove the sage leaves from the oil with a slotted spoon and drain it on paper towels. Add the shallots to the same pan, cover and sweat 2–3 minutes; don't let them caramelize. Add the orzo, spinach, butter, salt and pepper.

    Meanwhile, in another small sauté pan, heat the remaining tablespoon of olive oil. Place the proscuitto-wrapped sweetbreads in the pan and sear them lightly on each side (1–2 minutes).

TO SERVE. Place a 3 inch ring mold in the center of a serving plate. Spoon $\frac{1}{4}$ of the orzo mixture into each mold, pat down, then remove the mold. Place one sweetbread on top of the orzo mixture and spoon the sage-veal reduction over the top. Garnish with the fried sage leaves.

# SOUPS

**OLATHE SWEET CORN SOUP**
*Rock Shrimp, Avocado, Chili Oil*

**CREAMY GARLIC BISQUE**
*Seared Diver Scallop, Brioche Crouton*

**KABOCHA SQUASH SOUP**
*Pumpkin Seed Oil, Nutmeg Crema*

**French Onion Soup**
*Toasted Brioche Crouton, Appenzeller Swiss Fondu*

**SPRING PEA SOUP**
*Crab Cake Crouton*

**COLORADO HEIRLOOM TOMATO GAZPACHO**
*Manchego and Yellow Tomato Salsa*

# OLATHE SWEET CORN SOUP
*Rock Shrimp, Avocado, Chili Oil*
Serves 4

### SOUP

6 ears white corn with husks

1 tablespoon olive oil

1 cup yellow diced onion

1 cup diced celery

3 cloves garlic, minced

1 large Idaho potato, diced

1/4 cup white wine

1 bay leaf

Preheat the grill. Place the corn on the grill and let roast for 20 minutes over medium high heat, turning every 5 minutes. Remove the corn from the grill and place in a plastic bag to steam in the husk until cool.

Place the olive oil in a large pot over high heat. When the oil is hot, add the onion, celery and garlic, reduce heat slightly, cover and sweat about 10 minutes. Husk the corn and cut the kernels from the cob. Reserve 1 cup of the kernels for soup garnish. Return the heat to high and place the corn and the potatoes in the pot. Deglaze the pot with the white wine and then add enough water to cover the ingredients by 1 inch. Add the bay leaf, bring to a boil, reduce heat, and simmer 30 minutes. Cool.

Strain the liquid from the soup and reserve it. Place the vegetables in a blender and add back just enough liquid to purée. Strain the puréed vegetables through a chinois. Repeat the process with any remaining vegetables. Reheat the soup and season it to taste with salt and white pepper. You may need to add more of the reserved cooking liquid if the soup is too thick.

### GARNISH

1 tablespoon olive oil

1 tablespoon minced shallots

1 tablespoon minced garlic

1/2 pound rock (or any small) shrimp

1 avocado, diced

1 teaspoon fresh lime juice

salt and white pepper

chili oil (see recipe page 165)

Heat the olive oil in a small sauté pan over high heat. Add the shallots and garlic, cover and sweat 2 minutes Add the shrimp and cook until it's opaque, about 3 minutes. Transfer the mixture to a small bowl, and cool to room temperature. Add the avocado, reserved corn kernels and lime juice. Season with salt and pepper.

**TO SERVE.** Place a small ring mold in the center of each of 4 soup bowls. Divide the corn mixture evenly among the ring molds and gently press it down with the back of a spoon. Ladle the soup around the ring molds and then gently remove the molds. Drizzle the chili oil around the soup and serve immediately.

## CREAMY GARLIC BISQUE
*Seared Diver Scallop, Brioche Crouton*
Serves 4

### SOUP

      3 heads garlic, peeled, thinly sliced

      1 tablespoon olive oil

      1 cup diced yellow onion

      1 cup diced celery

      2 jars clam juice, 8 ounces each

      2 cups water

      1 cup heavy cream

      1 large potato, peeled and diced (about 2 cups)

      sachet d'epices (see recipe page 161)

      salt and white pepper

      sherry vinegar

Fill a small pot with water and bring it to a boil. Add the garlic and blanch for 1 minute, drain. Repeat blanching process.

    Place a medium size pot over high heat and add the oil. When the oil is hot, add the onions and celery, reduce heat to low, cover and sweat until tender, about 10 minutes. Deglaze the pot with the clam juice. Add the water, cream, potato and sachet d'epices. Bring to a boil, reduce heat and simmer until the potatoes are tender. Add the blanched garlic, and simmer another 5 minutes. Let cool. Purée the mixture in small batches in the blender. Strain through a chinois. Reheat the soup and season to taste with salt, pepper and sherry vinegar.

### GARNISH

      2 tablespoons butter

      4 squares Brioche, cut the same size as the scallops (see recipe page 165)

      4 large scallops, drained and patted dry with paper towels

      chive oil (see recipe page 163)

Heat the butter in a small sauté pan. Add the brioche squares and toast them until they are golden on each side.

    Wipe out the sauté pan and place it over high heat. Season the scallops with salt and pepper and sear them in dry sauté pan, about 2 minutes per side until golden brown.

**TO SERVE.** Place a brioche crouton in each bowl with a scallop resting on top. Gently ladle the soup around the crouton (it will appear as though the scallop is floating in the soup). Drizzle a little chive oil around the soup.

# KABOCHA SQUASH SOUP
*Pumpkin Seed Oil, Nutmeg Crema*
Serves 5

## NUTMEG CREMA

   2 tablespoons buttermilk

   1 cup heavy cream

   $\frac{1}{2}$ teaspoon nutmeg

Place all of the ingredients in a small bowl and whisk to incorporate. Set the mixture in a warm spot for 24–48 hours until it has thickened. Whisk again, then refrigerate for 24 hours before using.

## PUMPKIN SEED OIL

   1 cup pumpkin seeds, toasted

   1 cup olive oil

Purée the pumpkin seeds and oil in a blender. Let rest overnight. Strain before using.

## SOUP

   1 tablespoon olive oil

   1 cup diced yellow onion

   1 cup diced celery

   1 cup diced carrots

   8 cups peeled, seeded and diced kabocha squash

   $\frac{1}{4}$ cup white wine

   1 cup peeled and diced Idaho potato

   1 tablespoon minced marjoram

   salt and white pepper

Heat the olive oil in a large stockpot. Add the onion and celery, cover and sweat until translucent, about 10 minutes. Add the carrots and squash, cover and sweat the vegetables 10 more minutes. Deglaze the pot with white wine, then add the potato, marjoram and enough water to cover the ingredients. Bring the soup to a boil, reduce the heat and simmer until the potato and squash are tender (about 30 minutes). Let cool. Purée the soup in a blender in small batches, then strain through a chinois. Reheat and season with salt and pepper.

TO SERVE. Ladle hot soup into serving bowls. Drizzle with pumpkin seed oil and top with a dollop of nutmeg crema.

# FRENCH ONION SOUP
## *Toasted Brioche Crouton, Appenzeller Swiss Fondu*
Serves 4

| | |
|---|---|
| 2 tablespoons olive oil | 1 cup sliced shallots |
| 4 cups sliced yellow onion | 1 tablespoon sherry |
| 4 cups sliced red onion | 2 tablespoons butter |
| $1/3$ cup sliced garlic | salt and white pepper |

Heat the oil in large sauté pan. Add the onions and sauté until they begin to caramelize. Reduce the heat, add the garlic and shallots and continue to cook until the mixture is dark mahogany in color, about $1^{1}/_{2}$ hours. You may need to add a little water periodically to release all the browned bits on the bottom of the pan. Deglaze with the sherry, add the butter and season with salt and pepper. Keep warm.

### APPENZELLER SWISS FONDU

| | |
|---|---|
| 1 tablespoon butter | $^{3}/_{4}$ cup heavy cream |
| 1 shallot, minced | 2 cups grated Appenzeller swiss cheese (or gruyere) |
| $^{1}/_{4}$ cup white wine | salt and white pepper |

Melt the butter in a sauté pan. Add the shallots, cover and sweat, 1–2 minutes until tender. Deglaze with the wine and reduce by half. Add the cream and reduce by $^{1}/_{3}$. Whisk in the cheese until the mixture is thick and creamy. Season with salt and pepper, and then cool slightly. Purée the mixture in the blender and reheat in a double boiler. Form into 4 quenelles.

### BRIOCHE CROUTON

brioche, (see recipe page 165)

2 tablespoons butter

Cut the brioche into 4 slices ($^{1}/_{2}$ inch thick) and then cut a circle out of each slice with a 3 inch ring mold. Heat the butter in a small sauté pan and toast the brioche circles on each side.

### GARNISHES

2 tablespoons chives, thinly sliced

4 cups hot clarified veal stock (see recipe page 158)

TO SERVE. Place the ring mold in the center of the soup bowl and fill it half way with the onions. Pack down lightly with the back of a spoon and remove ring. Top with the crouton, cheese quenelle, and chives. Serve the broth hot in a separate container and pour table side.

# SPRING PEA SOUP
## *Crab Cake Crouton*
Serves 4

> 1 tablespoon olive oil
>
> 1 cup diced yellow onion
>
> 1 cup julienned leeks (white part only)
>
> 3 cups freshly shucked peas (about 3 pounds in shell)
>
> 2 cups chicken stock (see recipe page 159)
>
> salt and white pepper

Place a sauce pot over high heat and add the oil. When the oil is hot add the onions and leeks and sweat until translucent. Add the peas and stock, bring to a boil, then reduce the heat to low and simmer 10 minutes. Remove the pot from the stove and let cool. Strain out the liquid and reserve. Place the peas in the blender and add enough of the reserved liquid to make the pea purée into a soup consistency. Bring the soup back to a simmer and season with salt and pepper.

### CRAB CAKE CROUTON

> 3 slices fresh brioche, crusts removed (see recipe page165)
>
> 1 cup jumbo lump crab meat
>
> ½ cup roasted garlic aïoli (see recipe page 161)
>
> 1 teaspoon minced tarragon
>
> 1 teaspoon minced chervil
>
> salt and white pepper
>
> 2 tablespoons olive oil

Tear the bread into small pieces and feed one piece at a time in a running food processor, to make fresh bread crumbs. Place the remaining ingredients in a bowl and gently stir to combine evenly. Form into four 3 inch cakes. Heat the olive oil in a sauté pan large enough to hold the cakes without crowding. Add the cakes and brown on each side.

### GARNISH

> 1 tablespoon chives, minced

**TO SERVE.** Place one crab cake in the center of each soup bowl. Ladle the soup around the crab cake crouton or pour the soup into the bowls at tableside. Garnish with the chives.

# COLORADO HEIRLOOM TOMATO GAZPACHO
## *Manchego and Yellow Tomato Salsa*
Serves 4–6

8 Colorado heirloom tomatoes

1 large cucumber, peeled, seeded and finely diced

1 shallot, finely minced

1 clove garlic, finely minced

$\frac{1}{2}$ to 1 red jalapeno, brunoise, to taste

2 tablespoons sherry vinegar

2 tablespoon olive oil

1 tablespoon minced cilantro

1 tablespoon minced parsley

salt and white pepper

Bring a small pot of water to a boil. Core the tomatoes and cut an "x" in the bottom. Submerge 2 or 3 tomatoes at a time in the boiling water for 1 minute. Remove the from the water and place them in ice water. Peel the skin from the tomato. Repeat with the rest of the tomatoes. Place the tomatoes in a blender and purée. Strain through a chinois into a large bowl. Add the remaining ingredients and stir to combine. Chill for 1 hour.

### MANCHEGO AND YELLOW TOMATO SALSA

4 ounces manchego, diced

1 large yellow tomato, seeded and diced

2 tablespoons minced cilantro

2 tablespons olive oil

salt and white pepper

Combine all ingredients in a small bowl and chill.

TO SERVE. Ladle soup into serving bowls and top with salsa.

# SALADS

**RED AND YELLOW PICKLED BEETS**
*Haystack Mountain Goat Cheese Praline, Citrus Vinaigrette*

**MIZUNA SALAD**
*English Cucumbers, Roquefort, Champagne Vinaigrette*

**BLOOD ORANGE AND RED ONION SALAD**
*Watercress, Toasted Pine Nuts, Young Pecorino*

**CHILLED PRAWN SALAD**
*Marinated Baby Artichokes, Tomato Tartar, Basil Vinaigrette*

**HEARTS OF ROMAINE**
*White Anchovies, Roasted Garlic Peppercorn Dressing, Shaved Grana*

**GRILLED PALISADE PEACHES**
*Serrano Ham, Shaved Manchego*

# RED AND YELLOW PICKLED BEETS
*Goat Cheese Praline, Citrus Vinaigrette*
  Serves 8

## PICKLED BEETS

3 red beets

3 yellow beets

2-3 tablespoons olive oil

$\frac{1}{2}$ cup white wine vinegar

$\frac{1}{2}$ cup water

$\frac{1}{2}$ white onion, sliced

1 tablespoon honey

1 tablespoon mustard seed

$\frac{1}{4}$ teaspoon salt

Preheat the oven to 400°F. Trim the beet greens to a $\frac{1}{2}$ inch stem. Discard the greens. Toss the beets with olive oil and wrap them in foil. Place in the oven and roast 1 hour. Let cool, trim off ends, then peel and slice into $\frac{1}{4}$ inch slabs (you should have 5–6 slices per beet). Have 2 glass jars ready. (Canning jars work well.)

Combine vinegar, water, onion, honey, mustard seed and salt in a small sauce pan. Bring the mixture to a boil, reduce the heat and simmer 5 minutes.

Stack half of the beet slices in each jar. (Yellow in one, red in the other.) Pour half of the pickling liquid in each jar, then add the remaining beet slices. Place the lids on the jars, and shake gently to distribute pickling liquid evenly. Refrigerate overnight.

## CITRUS VINAIGRETTE

$\frac{1}{3}$ cup fresh orange juice

3 tablespoons fresh lemon juice

2 tablespoons fresh lime juice

1 tablespoon Dijon mustard

1 tablespoon honey

$\frac{1}{4}$ cup white wine vinegar

$\frac{3}{4}$ cup olive oil

salt and white pepper

8 cups mixed field greens

Place all of the ingredients except the oil and greens in a blender and purée. With blender running, slowly add the oil in a thin stream. Strain through a chinois then season with salt and white pepper. Place the greens in a large bowl and toss with $\frac{1}{2}$ cup of the dressing (more or less to taste).

## GOAT CHEESE PRALINE

1 cup finely ground toasted hazelnuts

8 ounce log of Hatstack Mountain goat cheese

Place the hazelnuts on a sheet of plastic wrap in an even layer the same as the width of the log of goat cheese. Roll the goat cheese in the hazelnuts. Roll the plastic wrap around the log and twist ends to tighten. Chill for 2 hours. Slice into 8 pieces.

**TO SERVE.** Divide the greens among 8 salad plates. Arrange the beet slices, alternating red and yellow, using 2 slices of each color beet on each plate. Place 1 slice of goat cheese praline on top.

## MIZUNA SALAD
*English Cucumbers, Roquefort, Champagne Vinaigrette*
Serves 8

Roquefort is a type of blue cheese that is made from sheeps milk and aged in the the limestone caverns of Mount Combalon in the south of France.

### DRESSING

> 1 tablespoon minced shallot
>
> $\frac{1}{4}$ cup champagne vinegar
>
> $\frac{3}{4}$ cup olive oil
>
> salt and white pepper

In a small bowl, combine the shallots, champagne vinegar and olive oil. Whisk briefly then add salt and pepper to taste.

### SALAD

> 8 cups field greens
>
> $\frac{1}{2}$ cup crumbled Roquefort
>
> 1 English cucumber, thinly sliced

**TO SERVE.** Toss the greens with the dressing to taste (about $\frac{1}{2}$ cup). Divide the greens evenly among 8 salad plates. Top with the Roquefort and sliced cucumber. Serve immediately.

# BLOOD ORANGE AND RED ONION SALAD
*Watercress, Toasted Pine Nuts, Young Pecorino*
Serves 4

### DRESSING

> 1 tablespoon minced shallots
>
> $\frac{1}{4}$ cup balsamic vinegar
>
> $\frac{3}{4}$ cup olive oil
>
> 1 teaspoon sugar
>
> salt and white pepper

In a small bowl, combine the shallots, vinegar, oil and sugar. Whisk to incorporate the ingredients evenly. Season with salt and pepper to taste.

### SALAD

> 2 blood oranges
>
> 2 hearts of frisée, cut each in half
>
> $\frac{1}{2}$ red onion, thinly sliced
>
> 4 ounces young pecorino, cut into chunks
>
> $\frac{1}{2}$ cup pine nuts, toasted
>
> basil oil (see recipe page 163)

TO SERVE. Cut the top and bottom from the blood oranges. Then slice off the outside peel and the outer membrane of the orange. Slice the oranges into $\frac{1}{2}$ inch thick slabs. Arrange 2–3 slices on each of four salad plates. Place a frisée half on top of the blood oranges. Top the frisée with a few slices of red onion. Drizzle the salad with 1–2 tablespoons of the dressing. Distribute the pecorino and pine nuts evenly among the plates. Drizzle the plate with a little basil oil.

# CHILLED PRAWN SALAD
## *Marinated Baby Artichokes, Tomato Tartar, Basil Vinaigrette*
Serves 6

### TOMATO TARTAR

> 6 large roma tomatoes, halved
>
> 6 cloves garlic, minced
>
> $\frac{1}{4}$ cup olive oil
>
> 2 tablespoons minced parsley
>
> $\frac{1}{4}$ cup chiffonade basil
>
> salt and white pepper

Preheat the oven to 175°F. Place all of the ingredients in a large bowl and toss to coat evenly. Place a wire rack on top of a baking sheet. Place the tomato halves on wire rack, cut side up. Place in the oven overnight, (12 hours), until tomatoes are dry. Put the tomatoes in a food processor and pulse until they are very finely minced.

### ARTICHOKES

> 4 cups water
>
> 1 cup white wine
>
> $\frac{1}{2}$ cup diced onion
>
> $\frac{1}{2}$ cup diced leeks
>
> $\frac{1}{2}$ cup diced carrots
>
> 2 sprigs thyme
>
> 2 bay leaves
>
> $\frac{1}{4}$ teaspoon salt
>
> 3 black peppercorns
>
> 9 baby artichokes, cleaned and quartered (see how to clean page 2)
>
> 1 pound extra large shrimp, peeled and deveined(16–20ct or 3 per person)

Place water, wine, onion, leek, carrots, thyme, bay leaves, salt and peppercorns in a large sauce pan. Bring the mixture to a boil then reduce the heat and simmer for 30 minutes. Add the artichokes and poach for 8–10 minutes until they are tender. Remove them from the poaching liquid with a slotted spoon and drain in a colander, leaving the cooking liquid in the pan. Add the shrimp to the pan and poach 8–10 minutes. Remove the shrimp with a slotted spoon and immediately place in ice water. Slice the shrimp in half lengthwise. Meanwhile, take half of the poached artichokes and toss in flour. Set aside until you are ready to serve. Preheat deep fryer to 375°F. When ready to serve, fry the artichoke hearts for 3 minutes until crispy. Drain on paper towels.

*—this recipe continues on the following page*

## BASIL VINAIGRETTE

> 1 cup packed basil leaves
>
> ½ cup packed spinach leaves
>
> 2 tablespoons minced shallot
>
> 1 tablespoon Dijon mustard
>
> 1 tablespoon white wine vinegar
>
> 2 teaspoons fresh lemon juice
>
> 2 teaspoons roasted garlic
>
> ½ cup whole milk
>
> salt and white pepper

Bring a small pot of water to a boil, add the basil and spinach and blanch 1–2 minutes. Then plunge them into ice water. Place all the ingredients, except the milk, in a blender. Slowly add the milk in a thin stream with the blender running. Strain the mixture through a chinois, season with salt and pepper to taste and pour into a squeeze tube.

## GARNISH

> ¼ cup aged balsamic vinegar

TO SERVE. Place a 3 inch ring mold in the center of each salad plate. Place 2 tablespoons tomato tartar into the mold and spread it into a thin even layer. Place 3 quarters of a poached artichoke heart in the center of the tomato tartar. Layer the shrimp in circles on top of the artichokes, cut side down. Top the shrimp with 3 fried artichoke quarters. Decorate the plate with descending size circles of basil vinaigrette and aged balsamic vinegar. (see photo on previous page)

# HEARTS OF ROMAINE
*White Anchovies, Roasted Garlic Peppercorn Dressing, Shaved Grana*

Serves 4

Grana is Italian for grain, referring to a variety of hard cheeses like Parmesan, that have been aged on the average of 2 to 7 years, but it can be much longer. They are best for grating. You can find pasteurized egg yolks in the dairy section of your grocery store.

## ROASTED GARLIC PEPPERCORN DRESSING

2 pasteurized egg yolks

1 tablespoon roasted garlic (see recipe page 162)

1 tablespoon red wine vinegar

1 teaspoon Worcestershire sauce

1 tablespoon fresh lemon juice

1 teaspoon black peppercorns, cracked

1 teaspoon Dijon mustard

$\frac{1}{2}$ cup olive oil

$\frac{1}{2}$ cup roasted garlic oil (see recipe page 162)

salt and white pepper

Place the egg yolks, garlic, vinegar, Worcestershire, lemon juice, peppercorns and mustard in the bowl of a food processor. Pulse until the egg yolks are pale yellow in color. With the food processor running slowly, add both of the oils in a thin stream. Season with salt and pepper to taste.

## SALAD

4 romaine hearts

$\frac{1}{4}$ cup shaved grana (Parmesan)

8 white anchovies

Coarsely chop the romaine hearts and place them in a large bowl Add the dressing to taste and toss with the romaine to coat it evenly.

**TO SERVE.** Divide the greens evenly among 4 salad plates. Top with shaved grana and white anchovies.

# GRILLED PALISADE PEACHES
## *Serrano Ham, Shaved Manchego*
Serves 4

Manchego is a Spanish cheese famous because it originally came from the milk of sheep that grazed on the plains of La Mancha.

### DRESSING

> 1 tablespoon finely minced shallot
>
> 1 tablespoon fresh lemon juice
>
> 1 tablespoon sherry vinegar
>
> 1 tablespoon honey
>
> $\frac{1}{4}$ cup olive oil
>
> salt and white pepper

Whisk all of the dressing ingredients together in a small bowl. Season with salt and pepper to taste.

### SALAD

> 4 small ripe Palisade peaches
>
> $\frac{1}{4}$ pound Serrano ham, thinly sliced
>
> $\frac{1}{4}$ pound manchego cheese
>
> 1 cup microgreens

Fill a small pot with water and bring it to a boil. Cut an "x" in the bottom of each peach and drop them in the boiling water for 1 minute. Remove them from the water and drop them into ice water. Peel the peaches, remove the seed and cut into quarters. Wrap each quarter peach with a slice of Serrano ham, then place them on a hot grill for about 3 to 5 minutes.

### GARNISH
Slice the manchego into strips with a vegetable peeler.

**TO SERVE.** Arrange 4 peach quarters on the salad plates in a star shape. Top the peaches with the microgreens. Drizzle the plate with the dressing and top with manchego shavings.

# SEAFOOD

### PAN SEARED ARCTIC CHAR
*Fava Bean Spaetzle, Braised Baby Leeks, Red Wine Sauce*

2001 Hartford Court "Marin" Pinot Noir

### PAN ROASTED CHILEAN SEA BASS
*Sweet Corn and Brioche Bread Pudding, Truffle Coulis, Tarragon Beet Relish*

2000 Hugel "Tradition" Pinot Gris

### PAN ROASTED BLACK COD
*Parsnip Purée, Lobster Champagne Velouté, Roasted Chanterelles*

2002 Marc Colin "Narvaux" Meursault

### MISO ROASTED HALIBUT
*Soy Glazed Peas and Carrots, White Truffle Sauce*

2002 Cold Heaven "Vogelsang" Viogner

### GRILLED OPAH
*Summer Vegetable Ratatouille, Caper Aïoli*

2002 Betts and Scholl Grenache

### GRILLED JUMBO PRAWNS
*Potato Gnocchi, Wilted Spinach, Toasted Garlic and Meyer Lemon Oil*

2003 Silvio Jermann's "Capo Martino"

### WILD KING SALMON
*Crème Fraîche Mashers, Poached Asparagus, Lemon Beurre Fondu, Chive Oil*

2002 Dutton-Goldfield "Dutton" Chardonnay

### SEARED MEXICAN JUMBO DIVER SCALLOPS
*Shrimp Toast, Roasted Red Pepper Bisque, English Pea Tendril Salad*

2003 Leeuwin Estate Riesling

### GREEN TEA POACHED STURGEON
*Farmer's Market Stir Fry, Spicy Carrot Sauce*

2003 Hofstaffer "Kolbenhof" Gewurztraminer

### PARMA PROSCIUTTO WRAPPED YELLOWFIN TUNA
*White Bean Croquette, Braised Baby Leeks, Veal Demi-Glace*

2001 Felsina Chianti Classico

# PAN SEARED ARCTIC CHAR
## *Fava Bean Spaetzle, Braised Baby Leeks, Red Wine Sauce*
### Serves 4

Spaetzle is german for little sparrow, and these little dumplings are usually boiled and then reheated in butter before serving.

### SPAETZLE

>1 bunch cilantro
>
>1 cup fava beans
>
>$2\frac{1}{4}$ cups flour
>
>$\frac{1}{2}$ teaspoon baking powder
>
>$\frac{1}{8}$ teaspoon nutmeg
>
>3 eggs, beaten
>
>$\frac{1}{2}$ cup water
>
>2 tablespoons butter
>
>salt and white pepper

Place a small pot of water over high heat. When it comes to a boil, add the cilantro and blanch it 1 minute until it is bright green. Immediately transfer it to a bowl of ice water. Drain the cilantro, chop roughly and place in a blender. Add just enough water to purée, about $\frac{1}{2}$ cup. Purée then strain through a chinois. Set aside. Do the same with the fava beans.

In a small bowl mix together the flour, baking powder and nutmeg. In another bowl combine the cilantro purée, fava bean purée, eggs and water. Slowly add to the flour mixture, whisking until smooth. Let rest 30 minutes.

Bring a large pot of water to a boil and push the spaetzle mixture (about a cup at a time) through a spaetzle maker into the water. Bring the water back to a boil and let it cook 3 minutes. Remove the spaetzle from the water with a slotted spoon or spider and shock in ice water. Repeat the process until all the batter has been used. Toss spaetzle with a little olive oil and spread in an even layer on a baking sheet until ready to use. When ready to serve, reheat in a large sauté pan with butter, salt and pepper.

### ROASTED MUSHROOMS

>8 ounces wild mushrooms
>
>$\frac{1}{3}$ cup olive oil
>
>3 tablespoons red wine vinegar
>
>salt and white pepper

Preheat the oven to 400°F. Toss all of the ingredients together in a small bowl. Spread the mushrooms in an even layer on a baking sheet and roast 25–30 minutes until golden. Remove from the oven and toss with the spaetzle.

*—this recipe continues on the following page*

## RED WINE SAUCE

    3 cups red wine

    1 cup peeled and diced carrots

    1 cup veal stock (see recipe page 158)

    salt and white pepper

    2 tablespoons butter

Combine the wine, carrots and stock in a small sauce pot. Bring to a boil, reduce to simmer and let the mixture reduce by half. Strain and reserve the carrots and the sauce separately. Place the carrots in a blender and add enough stock to purée. Strain the carrot purée through a chinois then pour back into the sauce pan. Reheat and season with salt and pepper. Just before serving slowly whisk in the butter.

## BRAISED BABY LEEKS

    4 baby leeks

    1 tablespoon olive oil

    $\frac{1}{4}$ cup white wine

    1 tablespoon butter

    salt and white pepper

Trim the green part from the leeks. Slice them in half lengthwise and rinse out any dirt, then chiffonade. Heat a small saucepan over high heat. Add the olive oil and when the oil is hot add the leeks. Sauté 2 minutes, deglaze with white wine, reduce heat, cover and braise 5–8 minutes until the leeks are tender. Add the butter and season with salt and pepper, keep warm until ready to serve.

## ARCTIC CHAR

    2 tablespoons olive oil

    $1\frac{1}{2}$ pounds arctic char, cut into 4 equal pieces

    salt and white pepper

Place a large sauté pan over high heat and add the olive oil. Season the fish with salt and pepper. When pan and oil are hot, add the fish flesh side down. Let it sear 3 minutes. Turn the fish over and finish cooking on the skin side, 3 more minutes.

**TO SERVE.** Divide the spaetzle mixture evenly among 4 serving plates. Place the fish on top of the spaetzle and top the fish with the braised leeks. Spoon the red wine sauce around the plate

## PAN ROASTED CHILEAN SEA BASS
*Sweet Corn and Brioche Bread Pudding, Truffle Coulis, Tarragon Beet Relish*
Serves 4

We know Chilean Sea Bass is a touchy subject, but we love the fish, and you can substitute halibut.

### TRUFFLE COULIS

>1 tablespoon olive oil
>
>1 small leek, julienned
>
>1 shallot, minced
>
>$\frac{1}{4}$ cup white wine
>
>1 cup milk
>
>4 tablespoons truffle peelings
>
>2 tablespoons butter, softened
>
>1 tablespoon truffle oil
>
>salt and white pepper

Heat the olive oil in a small saucepan. Add the leek and the shallot, cover and sweat until translucent, 2–3 minutes. Deglaze with the wine. Add the milk and truffle peelings and bring to a boil. Reduce the heat and simmer 5 minutes. Let the mixture cool to room temperature, then pour into a blender. Purée, then add the butter and truffle oil. Purée until it is black and emulsified. Reheat right before serving, but do not boil. Season with salt and pepper.

### TARRAGON BEET RELISH

>2 small beets
>
>2 tablespoons olive oil
>
>2 tablespoons minced shallots
>
>1 tablespoon minced tarragon
>
>1 teaspoon sherry vinegar
>
>salt and white pepper

Preheat the oven to 350°F. Trim the beet greens to within 1 inch of the top of the beet. Coat the beets with 1 tablespoon of the olive oil. Place them on a sheet tray, place in the oven and roast until tender (about 1 hour). Remove the beets from the oven and let cool. Peel the beets then cut them into a very small dice. Meanwhile, heat the remaining 1 tablespoon of olive oil in a small sauté pan. Add the shallots and sweat, 1–2 minutes, until translucent. Let cool then add to the beets. Add the tarragon and vinegar, toss and season with salt and pepper to taste.

*—this recipe continues on the following page*

## CHILEAN SEA BASS

    2 tablespoons olive oil

    $1\frac{1}{2}$ pounds Chilean sea bass, cut into 4 equal portions

    salt and white pepper

Preheat the oven to 400°F. Heat the olive oil in a large sauté pan over high heat. Season the fish with salt and pepper. When the pan is hot, carefully place the fish in the pan. Let sear 3–4 minutes until evenly browned. Turn the fish over. Place the pan in the oven. Finish roasting about 5–8 minutes, depending on the thickness of the fish.

## BREAD PUDDING

    1 tablespoon butter

    1 shallot, minced

    1 cup corn kernels (about 2 medium ears), blanched

    2 cups $\frac{1}{4}$ inch diced brioche (see recipe page 165)

    $\frac{1}{2}$ cup beurre blanc (see recipe page 162)

    $\frac{1}{4}$ cup heavy cream

    freshly grated nutmeg

    salt and white pepper

Melt the butter in a medium sauté pan over medium high heat. Add the shallot and sweat, about 2–3 minutes. Add the corn and heat through. Add the brioche cubes, $\frac{1}{4}$ cup of the beurre blanc and the cream. Cover and let cook until the bread is saturated. Remove the cover and season with the nutmeg, salt and pepper.

TO SERVE. Place a 3-inch ring mold in the center of each serving plate. Fill the mold with the bread pudding and pack it down lightly. Remove the ring mold. Place the fish on top of the bread pudding. Drizzle the fish with the remaining $\frac{1}{4}$ cup of the beurre blanc. Spoon the beet relish around the plate.

# PAN ROASTED BLACK COD
## *Parsnip Purée, Lobster Champagne Velouté, Roasted Chanterelles*
Serves 4

Black cod is also knows as sablefish. It is found in the pacific North West and has a delicate white meat. If you can't find it, substitute halibut.

### PARSNIP PURÉE

> 1 tablespoon olive oil
>
> $\frac{1}{2}$ cup diced yellow onion
>
> 2 large parsnips, peeled and diced
>
> salt and white pepper
>
> 2 tablespoons butter

Heat the olive oil in a small saucepan over medium high heat. Add the onion and sweat, 2–3 minutes, until translucent. Add the parsnips to the onion and cover them with water. Bring to a boil, reduce the heat and simmer until tender, about 30 minutes, and drain. Process the parsnips and onion through a food mill and season with salt and pepper. When ready to serve, melt the butter in a small sauté pan, add the parsnip purée and heat through.

### LOBSTER CHAMPAGNE VELOUTÉ

> 8 ounces butter (2 sticks)
>
> 4 lobster bodies, shells only
>
> 2 tablespoons tomato paste
>
> $\frac{3}{4}$ cup flour
>
> 2 cups champagne
>
> 6 cups water
>
> $\frac{1}{2}$ cup heavy cream
>
> salt and white pepper

Melt the butter in a large stockpot. Add the lobster shells and sauté them until they are bright red, about 10 minutes. Mash the shells with a wooden spoon as you cook them. Add the tomato paste and keep cooking until it caramelizes, about 5 minutes more. Add the flour and cook, stirring, 5–8 more minutes. Deglaze with the champagne. Add the water and cream, bring to a boil, reduce heat and simmer 1 hour until the sauce begins to thicken. It is important to stir the pot often and to scrape up all the browned bits from the sides and bottom of the pan. Let the sauce cool, remove the large pieces of shell, then purée in small batches in the blender and strain through a chinois. Reheat and season to taste with salt and pepper.

### PAN ROASTED BLACK COD AND ROASTED CHANTERELLES

1½ pounds black cod, cut into 4 equal portions

salt and white pepper

2 tablespoons olive oil

½ pound chanterelles

¼ cup white wine

Preheat the oven to 400°F. Season the fish with salt and pepper. Heat the olive oil in a large sauté pan. When the oil is hot add the black cod and sear for 3–4 minutes. Turn the fish over, add the chanterelles and deglaze with the wine. Place pan in the oven and finish cooking (3–4 minutes more).

TO SERVE. Fill a 3 inch ring mold with parsnip purée in the center of each plate. Remove the ring mold and place a piece of black cod on top of the purée. Top the fish with the mushrooms and ladle champagne velouté around the plate.

# MISO ROASTED HALIBUT
*Soy Glazed Peas and Carrots, White Truffle Sauce*
### 4 servings

Miso is fermented soy bean paste. White is the mildest form of miso. You can find it in the Asian food section in specialty grocery stores.

## WHITE TRUFFLE SAUCE

> 1 cup buerre blanc (see recipe page 162)
>
> 1 tablespoon truffle oil

Make the buerre blanc and whisk in the truffle oil.

## SOY GLAZED PEAS AND CARROTS

> 1 pound carrots
>
> 1 cup shucked fresh peas
>
> 2 tablespoons butter
>
> 1 tablespoon soy sauce

Peel the carrots. Using a small parisienne scoop (smaller than a melon ball scoop) cut out pea-sized scoops of carrot. They should be the same size as your shucked peas. Blanch the peas and carrots separately until just tender. When you are ready to serve, melt the butter in a sauté pan, add the peas and carrots, and heat through. Add the soy sauce.

## MISO ROASTED HALIBUT

> 4 tablespoons white miso
>
> 3–4 tablespoons water
>
> 1½ pounds halibut, cut into 4 equal portions
>
> 2 tablespoons olive oil
>
> 1 large Idaho potato, peeled and thinly sliced
>
> cilantro oil (see recipe page 164)
>
> microgreens

Preheat the oven to 500°F. Mix the miso and water to a thin even consistency. Brush the miso mixture on top of the halibut filets. Heat the oil in a large sauté pan over high heat. (The pan should be large enough to hold the fish without crowding.) Place the potato slices in the pan and place the halibut filets on top of the potatoes. Place the pan in the oven and roast 5–8 minutes, depending on the thickness of the filets, until flesh is opaque.

TO SERVE. Place a 3 inch ring mold in the center of each plate. Fill the mold with the pea mixture. Press down on the pea mixture with the back of a spoon. Carefully remove the ring mold. Place the halibut on top of the pea and carrots, top the fish with truffle sauce. Drizzle the plate with the cilantro oil. Top the fish with the microgreens.

# GRILLED OPAH
## *Summer Vegetable Ratatouille, Caper Aïoli*
Serves 6

Opah is a large round fish, caught in warm water and sold like tuna. The flesh is firm in texture, pink before cooking and white after.

## CAPER AÏOLI

¼ cup capers, minced

1 cup aïoli (see recipe page 161)

Stir the minced capers into the aioli and refrigerate until ready to serve.

## RATATOUILLE

1 tablespoon olive oil

1 large leek, cleaned and juilienned (white part only)

½ red onion, juilienned

2 cloves garlic, minced

2 small zucchini, diced

2 small yellow squash, diced

1 can diced tomatoes (28 ounce)

¼ cup chiffonade basil

1 teaspoon chili flakes

2 tablespoons butter

salt and white pepper

Place the olive oil in a large sauté pan over high heat. Add the leek and red onion, reduce the heat, cover and sweat the vegetables 8-10 minutes until tender. Add the garlic and cook another 2 minutes. Add the zucchini and yellow squash and cook until tender about (10–12 minutes). Add the diced tomatoes and cook another 5 minutes. Just before serving add the basil, chili flakes, and butter. Season with salt and pepper.

## GRILLED OPAH

2¼ pounds opah, cut into 6 equal portions

1 small eggplant, sliced, ½ inch thick (you will need 12 slices)

2 tablespoons olive oil

salt and white pepper

1 small eggplant, peeled and diced

½ cup flour

6–8 whole large basil leaves

basil oil (see recipe page 163)

Preheat the grill and deep fryer to 400°F. Season the fish and the eggplant slices with olive oil, salt and pepper. Toss the diced eggplant in a small bowl with flour.

Grill the fish about 3–4 minutes per side and the eggplant slices 1–2 minutes per side. Deep fry the diced eggplant and drain on paper towels. Season with salt and pepper. Deep fry the basil leaves until crisp, about 1 minute.

TO SERVE. Place one slice of grilled eggplant in the center of each plate. Fold the fried eggplant into the ratatouille, then top the grilled eggplant with about ½ cup of the ratatouille. Top with another slice of grilled eggplant. Top the second slice with the opah and put a small dollop of caper aïoli on top of the fish. Place one fried basil leaf into the caper aïoli and drizzle the plate with basil oil.

# GRILLED JUMBO PRAWNS
## Potato Gnocchi, Wilted Spinach, Toasted Garlic and Meyer Lemon Oil
Serves 6

Meyer Lemons were imported into the US in 1908 from China, and are believed to be a cross between lemons and oranges. They are slightly sweeter than lemons and are available November through May.

### GNOCCHI

> 2 Idaho potatoes
>
> 2 egg yolks
>
> 1 cup flour
>
> salt and white pepper
>
> 1 tablespoon olive oil
>
> 1 cup lobster stock (see recipe page 161)
>
> 4 tablespoons butter

Preheat the oven to 350°F. Prick the potatoes with a fork, place them in the oven and bake until very tender, about $1\frac{1}{2}$ hours. Remove them from the oven and let it cool. Peel the potatoes and cut them in half,and place them in a ricer. Push the potatoes through the ricer onto a flat work surface. Make a well in the center of the riced potatoes. Place the egg yolks and half of the flour ($\frac{1}{2}$ cup) in the center. Mix thoroughly with a pastry scraper, adding just enough of the remaining flour to bind the ingredients together, and form a smooth dough. Do not overmix. Too much flour or too much mixing will toughen the gnocchi. Form the dough into a ball and cut into four pieces. Roll each fourth into a snake about $\frac{1}{2}$ inch thick. Cut into $\frac{1}{2}$ inch pieces. Roll the pieces over the back of a fork to form gnocchi shape. Place the gnocchi on a parchment lined sheet tray and place in the freezer. When solid the gnocchi can be kept frozen for a couple of weeks in airtight plastic bags. To cook, bring a large pot of salted water to a boil. Cook the gnocchi in boiling water for 3–4 minutes, then drain in a colander.

When ready to serve, heat a large sauté pan over high heat. Add the olive oil then add the gnocchi. Sear the gnocchi on one side then flip them over. Add half of the lobster stock ($\frac{1}{2}$ cup) and let it reduce by half. Whisk in the butter. (You don't want the gnocchi to be crowded in the pan, so you may have to do two batches.) Heat remaining lobster stock in a small pot.

## GRILLED SHRIMP

    2 tablespoons olive oil

    1½ pounds large shrimp, peeled and deveined (about 24)

    2 tablespoons minced tarragon

    salt and white pepper

Preheat the grill. Coat the shrimp with the olive oil and tarragon, then season with salt and pepper. Sear on the grill about 3 minutes per side, depending on the size of the shrimp and the temperature of the grill. Shrimp should be opaque when cooked through.

## WILTED SPINACH

    2 bunches of spinach, washed, dried, stems removed

    2 tablespoons butter

    salt and white pepper

Bring a large pot of water to a boil. Blanch the spinach for 1 minute, then shock it in ice water. When ready to serve, melt the butter in a small sauté pan. Add the spinach and warm through. Season with salt and pepper.

## GARNISH

    ¼ cup toasted garlic and Meyer lemon oil (see recipe page 164)

**TO SERVE.** Divide the spinach into 6 serving bowls. For each person, place 8–10 gnocchi on top of the spinach. Arrange 4 shrimp around outside of the bowl, and pour enough of the remaining lobster stock into each bowl to just cover the bottom. Drizzle the toasted garlic and lemon oil around the broth.

## WILD KING SALMON
*Crème Fraîche Mashers, Poached Asparagus, Lemon Buerre Fondu, Chive Oil*
Serves 4

You will need to make the crème fraîche 2 days ahead.

### CRÈME FRAICHE

> 2 tablespoons buttermilk
>
> 1 cup heavy cream

Place the buttermilk and the cream in a glass jar with a tight fitting lid. Shake the mixture and leave it in a warm place overnight, or until thickened. Stir and refrigerate for 24 hours.

### MASHERS

> 4 large Idaho potatoes, peeled and diced
>
> salt and white pepper

Bring a large pot of water to a boil. Add the potatoes and simmer until tender, about 10 minutes. Drain and put through a food mill. Add the crème fraîche and mix thoroughly. Season with salt and pepper. Keep warm.

### LEMON BUERRE FONDU

> 1 cup buerre blanc (see recipe on page 162)
>
> 1–3 tablespoons fresh lemon juice

Make the buerre blanc and whisk in the lemon juice. Keep warm.

### MÂCHE SALAD

> 1 cup mâche greens
>
> 3 tablespoons olive oil
>
> 1 tablespoon fresh lemon juice
>
> salt and white pepper

Just before serving mix all ingredients together in a small bowl.

## SALMON

1 ½ pounds Wild King Salmon cut into 4 equal portions

1 bunch asparagus

chive oil (see recipe page 163)

salt and white pepper

Heat the olive oil in a large sauté pan. Season the salmon with salt and pepper. When the pan is hot, place the salmon in the pan, and sear on one side for 3 minutes. Turn the fish over and cook the other side 3 minutes or until salmon is medium-rare.

Meanwhile, bring a small pot of water to a boil, add the asparagus, and reduce the heat. Poach until the asparagus is just tender (3–5 minutes).

TO SERVE. Place a dollop of the mashers in the center of the plate. Top the mashers with a piece of salmon, and arrange the asparagus around the edge of plate end to tip. Top the fish with lemon buerre fondu and mâche salad. Drizzle the plate with chive oil.

# SEARED MEXICAN JUMBO DIVER SCALLOPS
*Shrimp Toast, Roasted Red Pepper Bisque, English Pea Tendril Salad*
Serves 4

You can find tendrils in specialty grocery stores and farmers markets in March, April and May.

## ENGLISH PEA TENDRIL SALAD

2 cups pea tendrils

1 carrot, peeled and grated

1 cup freshly shucked peas, blanched

1 tablespoon red wine vinegar

3 tablespoons olive oil

salt and white pepper

Mix all the ingredients together and chill.

## SHRIMP MOUSSE

1 tablespoon olive oil

1 shallot, minced

1 clove garlic, minced

1 pound shrimp, peeled and deveined

1 egg

1 tablespoon minced parsley

1 tablespoon minced tarragon

2 tablespoons heavy cream

salt and white pepper

Heat the olive oil in a small sauté pan. Add the shallot and garlic, cover and sweat, 2–3 minutes, until tender. Let cool. Place the shrimp, the cooled shallots and garlic, the egg, parsley and tarragon in the bowl of a food processor and purée. Add the heavy cream and pulse to incorporate. Be sure not to over-mix or you will whip the cream. Season with salt and pepper. Place the mixture in a pastry bag and chill.

*—this recipe continues on the following page*

## RED PEPPER BISQUE

> 1 tablespoon olive oil
>
> $\frac{1}{2}$ onion, diced
>
> 2 ribs celery, diced
>
> 4 red peppers, roasted, peeled, seeded, and diced
> (see method for roasting peppers page 167)
>
> 1 red pepper, seeded, diced
>
> $\frac{1}{2}$ cup diced Idaho potato
>
> $\frac{1}{4}$ cup white wine
>
> salt and white pepper

Heat the olive oil in a small pot. Add the onion and celery, cover and sweat, 2–3 minutes, until tender. Add all of the peppers and the potatoes and deglaze with the white wine. Add just enough water to cover the vegetables. Bring to a boil, reduce heat and simmer 20 minutes. Cool the mixture then purée in a blender. Strain through a chinois, reheat, and then season with salt and pepper.

## SEARED SCALLOPS AND SHRIMP TOAST

> $\frac{1}{2}$ loaf brioche (see recipe page 165)
>
> 16 large scallops (about $1\frac{1}{2}$ pounds)
>
> 4 tablespoons butter

Slice the brioche into four 1 inch thick slices. Cut out a 3 inch circle in each slice with a ring mold, then cut a 1 inch circle out of the center of the 3 inch circle and discard. Melt 2 tablespoons of the butter in a large sauté pan. Add the brioche, then pipe the center holes full of shrimp mousse. Toast the bread on each side about 3 minutes until the shrimp mousse is cooked through. Keep warm.

Heat a large sauté pan over high heat. When pan is very hot, carefully place the scallops, flat side down into the pan. Let them sear 3–5 minutes until browned. Turn the scallops over, reduce the heat and add the remaining 2 tablespoons of butter. Cook an additional 3 minutes until the scallops are opaque. Be sure not to add the butter too soon or it will burn, wait until the pan cools!

TO SERVE. Place one shrimp toast on each plate. Top with the tendril salad. Place 4 scallops on each plate. Alternately (between the scallops) place a spoonful of red pepper bisque on the plate. (see photo on previous page)

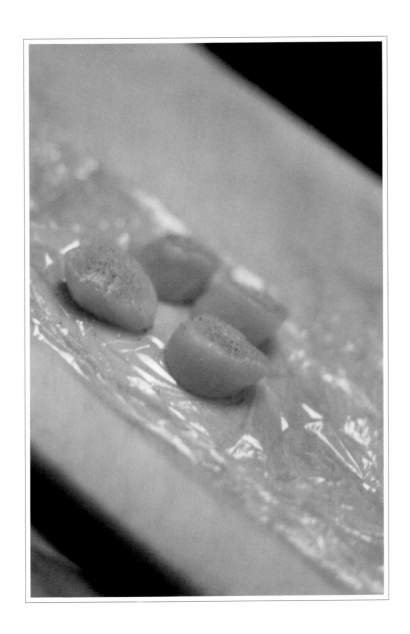

## GREEN TEA POACHED STURGEON
*Farmer's Market Stir Fry, Spicy Carrot Sauce*

4 servings

If you don't have a juicer, you can buy carrot juice in most grocery stores in the organic food section.

### STURGEON

6 green tea bags

1$\frac{1}{2}$ pounds halibut, cut into 4 equal portions

Place 6 cups of water in a wide shallow saucepan. Bring the water to a boil and add the tea bags. Turn off the heat and steep for 10–15 minutes. When almost ready to serve, bring the green tea back to a boil, add the fish, reduce heat to low and poach for 5–8 minutes.

### SPICY CARROT SAUCE

2 cups carrot juice (or use two pounds carrots and juice them)

1 teaspoon cayenne pepper

4 tablespoons butter, cut into small pieces

salt and white pepper to taste

Place the carrot juice and cayenne pepper in a small saucepan over high heat. Bring to a boil, reduce liquid by half. Turn heat to low. Add the butter one piece at a time and emulsify with a hand blender; keep warm.

## STIR FRY

  8 baby eggplant, cut into 2 inch batonnets

  2 tablespoons flour

  2 tablespoons sesame oil

  1 tablespoon minced garlic

  1 tablespoon minced ginger

  2 tablespoons minced scallions

  2 cups thinly sliced red cabbage

  2 cups julienned snap peas

  4 ounces mung sprouts

  1 tablespoon mirin

  1 tablespoon soy sauce

  salt and white pepper

Preheat the fryer to 375°F. Place the eggplant batonnets and flour in a small bowl and toss to coat. When ready to serve, fry the eggplant in 2–3 batches (depending on the size of your fryer), until they are golden brown. Drain them on paper towels and season with salt and pepper.

   Place a large sauté pan over high heat and add the sesame oil. When the pan is hot, add the garlic, ginger and scallions. Sauté 2–3 minutes until the mixture starts to color. Add the red cabbage and reduce the heat slightly. Cook 3–4 minutes, until the cabbage starts to soften. Add the snap peas and cook another 2 minutes then add the mung sprouts. Deglaze the pan with mirin and soy sauce. Season the mixture with salt and pepper. Keep warm.

TO SERVE. Divide the stir fry into 4 portions, placing it in the center of each plate. Carefully remove the fish from the poaching liquid with a large slotted spoon or spider. Place it on top of the stir fry. Top the fish with the fried eggplant and spoon carrot sauce around the edges of the plate.

# PARMA PROSCIUTTO WRAPPED YELLOWFIN TUNA
*White Bean Croquette, Braised Baby Leeks, Veal Demi-Glace*
Serves 6

You can form these croquettes a day ahead up to the breading point and freeze.

## WHITE BEAN CROQUETTES

$\frac{1}{2}$ cup white beans (that have been soaked overnight in water and drained)

2 tablespoons minced bacon

$\frac{1}{2}$ cup diced onion

$\frac{1}{2}$ cup diced celery

$\frac{1}{2}$ cup diced carrot

$\frac{1}{4}$ cup white wine

1 bay leaf

2 tablespoons minced oregano

2 large Idaho potatoes, cooked, peeled and diced

2 tablespoons butter, softened

2 egg yolks

salt and white pepper

1 cup flour

2 eggs beaten with 1 tablespoon water

1 cup panko (Japanese bread crumbs)

Place the beans in a pot and cover with water. Bring to a boil, drain and rinse.

Heat a small sauce pot over high heat and add the bacon, and cook until crispy. Drain off the excess fat; add the onion, celery and carrot. Reduce the heat and sweat the vegetables until they are tender, about 10 minutes. Add the beans, deglaze the pan with the white wine, and then add the bay leaf and oregano. Cover the beans by 1 inch with water and bring to a boil. Reduce the heat and simmer until the beans are very tender, about $1\frac{1}{2}$–2 hours. Drain the beans, reserving the liquid. Place the beans in the bowl of a food processor and purée until smooth.

Place the potatoes in a ricer and press them into a bowl. Add the bean purée, butter and egg yolks. Stir to incorporate evenly and season with salt and pepper. Shape the mixture into 2 inch long, $\frac{1}{2}$ inch round logs. Place on a parchment-lined baking sheet and chill or freeze the the logs 2 hours until firm. Place the flour, eggs and panko each in a separate bowl. Dip each log into the flour, then the egg wash, then the breadcrumbs. Freeze in an airtight container until ready to serve.

Preheat the deep fryer to 375°F. Fry each log 3–4 minutes until golden. Drain on paper-towel lined baking sheets.

### BRAISED BABY LEEKS

    3 tablespoons minced bacon

    6 baby leeks, cleaned and quartered

    $\frac{1}{4}$ cup white wine

Place a small sauce pot over high heat and add the bacon, cook until crispy. Drain the excess fat, then add the leeks and sauté 2–3 minutes. Deglaze the pan with the white wine, cover the pan, reduce the heat to low and let cook 15–20 minutes until the leeks are very tender. You may need to add a tablespoon of water during the cooking process if the pan gets dry.

### PROSCIUTTO WRAPPED TUNA

    6 slices Parma prosciutto

    $2\frac{1}{4}$ pounds yellowfin tuna cut into 6 equal portions

    salt and white pepper

    1 tablespoon olive oil

    1 cup hot veal demi-glace (see recipe page 158)

Lay the proscuitto slices flat on the work surface. Season the tuna with salt and pepper. Place one piece of tuna on each slice of the prosciutto and wrap it around. Heat the olive oil in a large sauté pan until very hot. Sear the tuna about 2 minutes per side. Heat the veal demi-glace in small sauce pan.

**TO SERVE.** Place 2 croquettes in the center of each plate. Top it with tuna, then the leeks. Drizzle the plate with veal demi-glace.

# — RED MEAT

## GRILLED BEEF TENDERLOIN
*Butternut Squash and Foie Gras Hash, Asparagus, Béarnaise*
2001 Caymus

## GRILLED BUFFALO RIB EYE
*Chorizo Braised Black Beans, Sweet Corn Crema*
2001 Montevina "Terra d'Oro" Zinfandel

## GRILLED COLORADO LAMB STRIP LOIN
*Spaghetti Squash Latkes, French Feta, Pickled Red Onion, Kalamata Olive Jus*
John Kongsgaard's 2002 Arietta Merlot

## GRILLED LAMB TENDERLOIN
*Braised Lamb and Potato Knish, Goat Cheese Vinaigrette*
2001 Pichon Lalande

## ROASTED PORK TENDERLOIN
*Fresh Buttermilk Biscuits, Bacon Braised Brussels Sprouts, White Cheddar Fondu*
2002 Dubreuil-Fontaine Beaune Montrevenots

## PORK SHOULDER CONFIT
*Butternut Squash Gratin, Wilted Collard Greens, Smoked Bacon Demi-Glace*
2002 Ehren Jordan's Syrah Lee Hudson Vineyard

## PAN SEARED VEAL CHOP
*Cauliflower Bread Pudding, Haricots Verts, Caramelized Shallot Sauce*
1991 Montecillo Rioja Gran Reserva

## RED WINE BRAISED VEAL CHEEKS
*Yukon Gold Potato Pirogi, Wilted Spinach, Caramelized Onions, Carrot Butter Purée*
2001 Rockford "Basket Press" Shiraz

## VEAL TENDERLOIN MEDALLIONS
*Carnaroli Risotto, Broccoli Rabe, Truffle Demi-Glace*
2000 Damilano Barolo

## BLACK PEPPER GRILLED VENISON LOIN
*Potato Fondant, Haricots Verts, Sun-Dried Cherry Jus*
Robert Jasmin's 1999 Cote-Rotie

# GRILLED BEEF TENDERLOIN
*Butternut Squash and Foie Gras Hash, Asparagus, Béarnaise*
Serves 4

This recipe is an enriched version of your traditional steak and potatoes.

## HASH

> 1 large butternut squash, peeled, seeded and diced $\frac{1}{2}$ inch x $\frac{1}{2}$ inch
>
> 3 tablespoons olive oil
>
> salt and white pepper
>
> 4 tablespoons diced foie gras
>
> 2 tablespoons chiffonade sage

Preheat the oven to 400°F. Place the squash in a large bowl and coat it with olive oil, salt and pepper. Place it on a sheet tray in an even layer and roast it in the oven for 20 minutes, until tender. Remove the squash from the oven and let it cool. When ready to serve, heat a large sauté pan over high heat. Add the foie gras and let it start to render. Add the roasted squash and sage chiffonade and heat through.

## BEEF

> 2 pounds beef tenderloin, trussed, cut into 4 equal portions
>
> olive oil
>
> salt and black pepper

Preheat the grill. Coat the tenderloin with oil, and season with salt and pepper. Place the meat on the grill and cook 5–6 minutes per side depending on the desired doneness and the thickness of the filet. Cover the meat and let it rest 10 minutes. Then remove the trussing.

## ASPARAGUS

> 1 bunch asparagus
>
> 1 tablespoon butter
>
> salt and white pepper

Trim the ends from the asparagus. Bring a large pot of water to a boil and blanch the asparagus until it is just tender, about 3 minutes. Remove the asparagus from the water and shock it in an ice bath. When you are ready to serve, melt the butter in a sauce pan and add the asparagus. Heat through then season with salt and pepper.

## BÉARNAISE

    1 shallot, minced

    2 black peppercorns, crushed

    $\frac{1}{4}$ cup white wine

    $\frac{1}{4}$ cup tarragon vinegar, (you can substitute white wine vinegar)

    3 egg yolks

    2 sticks butter, clarified (see method page 162)

    2 tablespoons minced tarragon

    salt and white pepper

Place the shallot, peppercorns, wine and vinegar in a small sauce pot. Bring to a boil and let reduce until there are only 2 tablespoons of liquid left. Strain out the shallots and peppercorns, reserving the liquid.

Heat a small sauce pot of water to boiling, then reduce to simmer. Place the egg yolks in a bowl and place the bowl on top of the simmering water. Whisk the egg yolks until they are thick and foamy. Add the reserved vinegar reduction. Continue whisking the egg yolks until they have thickened. Slowly add the clarified butter in a thin stream, while whisking the egg yolks constantly. The mixture should become the consistency of thin mayonnaise. Fold in the tarragon, season with salt and pepper and keep warm.

TO SERVE. On each plate fill a 3 inch ring mold with the foie gras hash. Gently pack it down with the back of a spoon, then remove the ring mold. Place 4–5 asparagus spears on each plate, next to the hash and place one portion of beef tenderloin on top of the ends of the asparagus. Drizzle the béarnaise over the beef and asparagus.

# GRILLED BUFFALO RIB EYE
## *Chorizo Braised Black Beans, Sweet Corn Crema*
Serves 6

Chorizo is a highly seasoned pork sausage used in Mexican and Spanish cooking.

### CHORIZO BRAISED BLACK BEANS

1 cup black beans, soaked in water overnight

1 small sweet potato

1 tablespoon olive oil

1 cup diced onion

1 cup diced celery

1 tablespoon minced garlic

1 pound chorizo, casing removed

1 tablespoon cumin

1 teaspoon chili powder

salt and white pepper

Drain the beans and place them in a small pot. Cover them with water. Bring the water to a boil then drain.

Peel the sweet potato and cut it into $1/2$ inch dice. You should get about 2 cups. Bring a small pot of water to a boil, add the sweet potato and cook it until just tender, 8–10 minutes.

Heat the oil in a large pot over medium high heat. Add the onion and celery, cover and sweat 8–10 minutes until the vegetables are tender. Add the garlic and cook 2 minutes. Add the chorizo and brown it. Drain off any excess fat, then add the black beans, cumin, chili powder and 2 cups of water (just enough to cover the beans). Bring the mixture to a boil, reduce the heat to simmer and cook about 2 hours until the beans are tender. You may need to add a little water, but don't add too much. You want most of the liquid to be absorbed when the beans are done. Just before serving add the sweet potatoes and season with salt and pepper.

## Sweet Corn Crema

6 ears sweet corn, shucked

1 tablespoon olive oil

1 large shallot, minced

1 tablespoon minced garlic

$\frac{1}{2}$ cup white wine

1 cup heavy cream

salt and white pepper

Bring a large pot of water to a boil. Add the corn and cook for 10 minutes. Shock the corn in ice water, then cut the kernels from the cob.

Heat the olive oil in a small sauce pan over medium high heat. Add the shallots and garlic, cover and sweat 2–3 minutes until tender. Deglaze with the wine, then add the corn and cream. Bring to a boil, reduce the heat and simmer 15 minutes. Cool. Purée the mixture in a blender, then strain through a chinois. Reheat and season with salt and pepper.

## Rib-Eyes

6 buffalo rib eyes (12 ounces each)

olive oil

salt and black pepper

chili oil (see recipe page 164)

Preheat the grill. Season the steaks with olive oil, salt and black pepper. Sear the steaks on the grill to the desired doneness. (Remember, buffalo is a game meat and is a little drier that beef, so it is better to cook it a little less than usual, we recommend no more than medium rare.) Remove the steaks from the grill, cover them and let them rest 10 minutes before serving.

TO SERVE. Place a 3 inch ring mold in the center of each plate. Fill with black beans and pack them down with the back of a spoon. Remove the mold. Ladle about 4 ounces ($\frac{1}{2}$ cup) of crema around the plate. Gently lean the steak on top of the beans and drizzle the plate with chili oil.

# GRILLED COLORADO LAMB STRIP LOIN
*Spaghetti Squash Latkes, French Feta, Pickled Red Onion, Kalamata Olive Jus*

Serves 6

This is a twist on the traditional shredded potato Latkes, served in Jewish households on Hanukkah.

## SPAGHETTI SQUASH LATKES

> 1 large spaghetti squash (about 4 cups after roasting)
>
> 2 tablespoons olive oil
>
> 1 large onion, diced
>
> 3 large Idaho potatoes, peeled and grated (about 4 cups)
>
> 5 eggs, slightly beaten
>
> 1 cup flour
>
> 1 teaspoon baking powder
>
> salt and white pepper
>
> 2 tablespoons olive oil

Preheat the oven to 350°F. Cut the spaghetti squash in half lengthwise and season the inside with 1 tablespoon of olive oil, salt and white pepper. Place the squash on a sheet tray cut side down, and put in the oven. Roast it for 45 minutes to an hour until fork tender. Remove the squash from the oven and let cool.

Meanwhile, heat the remaining tablespoon of olive oil in a small sauté pan over high heat. Add the onion, cover, and sweat 2–3 minutes then reduce the heat and sweat the onions until tender. Let cool.

Scrape the flesh out of the squash with the tines of a fork, and put into a large bowl. Add the onions and potatoes and mix thoroughly.

Add the eggs and mix again. Add the flour $\frac{1}{4}$ cup at a time, until there is no liquid left in the bowl, then add the baking powder, salt and pepper. Oil a large jelly roll pan ($15\frac{1}{2}$ x$10\frac{1}{2}$ x1 inches) and spread the latke mixture in an even layer. Bake until the mixture is firm in the center, about 45–55 minutes. Let cool slightly, then flip out of the pan onto a cutting board. Cut out circles with a 3 inch ring mold. Keep warm.

## PICKLED RED ONION (Make this part at least a day ahead.)

> 1 cup water
>
> 2 tablespoons sugar
>
> $\frac{1}{2}$ cup red wine vinegar
>
> 1 small red onion, diced

Place the water, sugar and red wine vinegar in a small pan over high heat. Bring the mixture to a boil and add the onion. Reduce the heat and simmer for ten minutes, until onions are tender but still have a slight crunch. Chill overnight.

*—this recipe continues on the following page*

## FETA SALAD

$\frac{1}{2}$ pound French feta, crumbled

1 heart of romaine, chiffonade

2–3 tablespoons olive oil

1–2 tablespoons fresh lemon juice

pickled red onion (previous recipe)

Mix all of the ingredients together and chill.

## KALAMATA OLIVE JUS

$\frac{1}{4}$ cup olive oil

2 tablespoons minced shallots

1 cup kalamata olives, pitted

2 Meyer lemons, juiced and zested

2 tablespoons balsamic vinegar

Place 1 tablespoon of the olive oil in a small sauce pan over medium high heat. Add the shallots, cover and sweat until tender. Add the olives, lemon juice and zest, vinegar and the remaining 3 tablespoons oil and turn heat to low. Let simmer 20–30 minutes, until reduced and slightly thickened.

## LAMB

3 pounds Colorado Lamb Strip Loin

olive oil

salt and black pepper

Preheat the grill. Season the lamb with olive oil, salt and black pepper. Cook the lamb to your desired temperature. Remove the lamb from the grill, cover and let rest 10 minutes. Slice the lamb on the bias in $\frac{1}{4}$ inch thick slices.

TO SERVE. Place one latke in the center of each plate. Top with a little feta salad and then top that with another latke and a little more feta salad. Fan out 4–5 slices of lamb in front of the latkes and place a few spoonfuls of kalamata olive Jus around edge of plate. (see photo previous page.)

# GRILLED LAMB TENDERLOIN
## *Braised Lamb and Potato Knish, Goat Cheese Vinaigrette*
Serves 6

You will want to braise the lamb and make the knishes a day ahead.

### BRAISED LAMB

> 1 tablespoon olive oil
>
> 1 lamb shank (approximately $1\frac{1}{4}$ pounds)
>
> salt and black pepper
>
> $\frac{1}{2}$ cup diced onion
>
> $\frac{1}{2}$ cup diced celery
>
> $\frac{1}{2}$ cup diced carrot
>
> 1 tablespoon minced garlic
>
> 1 tablespoon tomato paste
>
> $\frac{1}{4}$ cup white wine
>
> 1 cup lamb stock (see recipe page 158)
>
> 1 bay leaf
>
> 1 sprig rosemary

Heat the olive oil in a medium size pot. Season the lamb shank with salt and black pepper, and sear on all sides. Remove the lamb from the pot. Add the onion, celery and carrots, and sauté until they begin to caramelize. Add the garlic and tomato paste and sauté until they are fully caramelized. Deglaze the pan with the wine. Add the lamb shank, lamb stock, bay leaf and rosemary. Bring to a boil, reduce the heat to low, and simmer $1\frac{1}{2}$ hours until very tender. Let cool, then remove the meat from the bone. Reserve.

### POTATO KNISH

> 2 Idaho potatoes, peeled and diced
>
> 2 tablespoons butter
>
> $\frac{1}{4}$ cup heavy cream
>
> salt and white pepper
>
> reserved lamb meat (see previous recipe)
>
> $\frac{1}{2}$ cup flour
>
> 1 egg, beaten
>
> 2 cups Japanese bread crumbs (panko)
>
> 2–4 tablespoons olive oil

Cook the potatoes in water until they are tender. Mash them together with the butter and cream. Season with salt and pepper. Fold in the lamb meat. Make 6 knishes by forming patties that are 3 inches in diameter and $\frac{1}{2}$ inch thick. Place the flour, egg wash and bread crumbs in 3 separate bowls. Bread the knishes by coating them with the flour, then dipping in the egg wash, and then in the bread crumbs. You can make them up to this point a day ahead and chill overnight. When ready to serve, heat the olive oil in a large sauté pan or flat griddle. Place the knishes on the griddle and brown about 2–3 minutes per side.

## GOAT CHEESE VINAIGRETTE

> 1 cup soft crumbled Haystack Mountain goat cheese
>
> 1 tablespoon minced shallot
>
> $\frac{1}{4}$ cup white wine vinegar
>
> 1 tablespoon minced thyme
>
> $\frac{3}{4}$ cup olive oil
>
> salt and white pepper

Place all of the ingredients in a small bowl and whisk until smooth. Season with salt and pepper if needed.

## LAMB

> 3 lamb tenderloins
>
> olive oil
>
> salt and black pepper
>
> microgreens

Preheat the grill. Season the tenderloins with the olive oil, salt and pepper. Place the meat on a hot oiled grill and cook 3–5 minutes per side. Cover the meat and let it rest 10 minutes before serving. Slice it on the bias.

TO SERVE. Place a knish in center of each plate. Place slices of lamb around the knish (about half a tenderloin per person). Drizzle the goat cheese vinaigrette around outside of plate. Garnish with microgreens.

# ROASTED PORK TENDERLOIN
*Fresh Buttermilk Biscuits, Bacon Braised Brussels Sprouts, White Cheddar Fondu*
Serves 4

Brussels sprouts are said to be originally from Belgium. Choose the smallest ones you can find.

## PORK TENDERLOIN

2 pork tenderloins, about 1 pound each

olive oil

salt and black pepper

Preheat the charcoal grill. Season the pork with olive oil, salt and pepper. Place the tenderloin on the grill and sear on all sides. Move the pork off the direct heat and finish cooking (10–12 minutes), depending on the thickness of the tenderloin and the desired doneness. Remove the tenderloin from the grill, cover and let rest 10 minutes. Then slice on the bias, $\frac{1}{4}$ inch thick.

## BUTTERMILK BISCUITS

2 cups flour, plus more for dusting

1 tablespoon baking powder

1 teaspoon sugar

$\frac{1}{4}$ teaspoon salt

$\frac{1}{2}$ cup butter (1 stick), cut into small pieces

$\frac{3}{4}$ cup buttermilk

Preheat the oven to 425°F. Place the flour, baking powder, sugar and salt in the bowl of a standing mixer with the paddle attachment. Turn the mixer on low and add the butter pieces, one at a time. Mix until all of the butter is incorporated and the mixture looks like cornmeal. Add the buttermilk in a thin stream and mix until just incorporated. Remove the dough from the bowl and place it on a floured work surface. Knead the dough until it is smooth. Fold the dough in half to create layers in the biscuits. Shape into a rectangle about 3x4 inches that is about $\frac{1}{2}$ inch thick. Cut the outside edges, to even, then cut into 4 large biscuits. Bake about 12–15 minutes until edges are golden and center is done.

## BACON BRAISED BRUSSELS SPROUTS

    4 slices smoked bacon, julienned

    1 pound small Brussels sprouts, bottoms trimmed and outer leaves removed

    $\frac{1}{4}$ cup pork stock (see recipe page 158)

Place a saucepan over high heat and add the bacon. When the bacon begins to sizzle, add the Brussels sprouts and sauté a few minutes on high heat until the Brussels sprouts begin to brown. Add the pork stock, reduce the heat to low and cover. Cook 5–8 minutes until the Brussels sprouts are tender.

## WHITE CHEDDAR FONDU

    1 tablespoon olive oil

    1 tablespoon minced shallots

    $\frac{1}{4}$ cup white wine

    $\frac{1}{2}$ cup heavy cream

    1 cup white cheddar, grated

Place the olive oil in a small saucepot over medium high heat. Add the shallots, cover and sweat, 2-3 minutes until translucent. Deglaze with the wine and reduce by half. Add the cream and reduce that by half. Strain the mixture through a chinois to remove the shallots. Reheat, then add the cheddar and whisk until the mixture is smooth. Keep warm until ready to serve. You may need to add a tablespoon or so of water if it becomes too thick.

TO SERVE. Place a biscuit in the center of each plate. Arrange the pork slices in front of the biscuit and the Brussels sprouts in front of the pork. Pour the white cheddar fondu over the biscuit.

## PORK SHOULDER CONFIT
*Butternut Squash Gratin, Wilted Collard Greens, Smoked Bacon Demi-Glace*
6 servings

We have gone one step beyond the traditional confit and used pork instead of duck or goose.

### PORK SHOULDER CONFIT
You will need to start this part at least 2 days ahead.

> 1 cup salt
>
> $\frac{1}{2}$ cup sugar
>
> $\frac{1}{2}$ cup brown sugar
>
> 2 tablespoon crushed black peppercorns
>
> 1 tablespoon minced thyme
>
> 1 tablespoon minced sage
>
> 1 tablespoon minced rosemary
>
> 1 tablespoon minced marjoram
>
> 3 bay leaves
>
> 2 pounds pork shoulder, one large piece
>
> 12 cups duck fat

Place a large piece of cheesecloth on a sheet tray. Mix the salt, sugars, peppercorns, thyme, sage, rosemary, marjoram and bay leaves together. Coat the pork with the curing mixture. Place the pork on the cheesecloth. Wrap the pork in cheesecloth and let it rest overnight in the refrigerator (24 hours). Rinse the cure from the pork. Place the pork in a deep baking dish that is only slightly wider than the pork.

Preheat the oven to 275°. Place the duck fat in a pot over low heat. When the fat becomes liquid, pour it over the pork, making sure the pork is completely immersed in the fat. Bake for 6 hours. Let rest in the fat overnight or until ready to use. When ready to serve, warm the pork until the fat has liquefied and then remove the pork. Slice it $\frac{1}{2}$ inch thick.

—*this recipe continues on the following page*

## BUTTERNUT SQUASH GRATIN

>   2 tablespoons olive oil
>
>   4 small yellow onions, sliced thin
>
>   2 small butternut squash, peeled (tops only) seedy bottoms removed
>
>   2 large Idaho potatoes, peeled
>
>   2 cups heavy cream
>
>   salt and white pepper

Preheat the oven to 350°F. Heat the olive oil in a large sauté pan over high heat. Add the onions and sauté until they begin to caramelize. Turn the heat to medium low and continue to cook until the onions are uniformly dark brown in color. You may need to deglaze the pan a few times with water to remove all caramelized bits from the bottom of the pan. Let cool slightly. Slice the butternut squash tops and potatoes in a food processor. Let the potatoes rest in the cream until you are ready to layer in the baking pan so they don't turn brown. Place an even layer of each item in a 11x7x2 inch baking dish. Beginning with the squash, then the potatoes, then the onions, you should have enough for 2 layers of each. Press the mixture firmly into the pan. Cover with the cream, season with salt and pepper. Wrap the pan tightly with plastic wrap and then cover with foil. Place the pan in the oven and bake for 90 minutes. Uncover and bake another 15 minutes. Remove the dish from the oven and let it rest 15 minutes before cutting into 12 squares. You will have a few extra portions.

## WILTED COLLARD GREENS

>   1 pound collard greens
>
>   2 tablespoons butter

Bring a small pot of water to a boil. Remove any large stems from the collard greens. Place the greens in the boiling water for 2 minutes until bright green. Remove them from the boiling water and shock in ice water. When ready to serve, melt the butter in a small sauté pan, add the collard greens and heat through.

## SMOKED BACON DEMI-GLACE

>   6 slices smoked bacon, julienned
>
>   2 cup pork stock (see recipe page 158)

Place a small sauté pan over high heat. Add the bacon and cook until the bacon is crisp. Drain off the excess fat, add the pork stock and reduce by half.

**TO SERVE.** Place one gratin square in the center of each plate. Place the collard greens on edge of the gratin and rest the pork on the greens. Drizzle the plate with smoked bacon demi-glace.

# PAN SEARED VEAL CHOP
*Cauliflower Bread Pudding, Haricots Verts, Caramelized Shallot Sauce*
### Serves 6

## BREAD PUDDING
Cut the bread the night before and leave it out overnight on a baking sheet to dry.

> 5 slices texas toast, diced
>
> 1 tablespoon olive oil
>
> $\frac{1}{2}$ cup diced onion
>
> $\frac{1}{2}$ cup diced celery
>
> 1 tablespoon minced garlic
>
> 2 tablespoons minced thyme
>
> 4 eggs, beaten
>
> 1 cup milk
>
> $\frac{1}{2}$ head cauliflower florets, blanched

Preheat the oven to 350°F. Spray six ramekins (4 ounces each) with non-stick cooking spray. Heat the olive oil in a sauté pan. Add the onion, celery and garlic. Reduce the heat slightly, cover and sweat, 3–4 minutes until translucent. Be careful not to let the vegetables brown. Add the thyme and let cool. Combine the eggs and milk in a large bowl, fold in cauliflower florets, bread cubes and the onion mixture, season with salt and pepper. Spoon the mixture into the prepared ramekins (they should be $\frac{3}{4}$ full). Place the ramekins in a 13x9x2 inch baking pan and fill the pan half way with water. Bake for 40–45 minutes until a knife inserted in the center comes out clean.

## CARAMELIZED SHALLOT SAUCE

> 1 tablespoon olive oil
>
> 5 shallots, thinly sliced
>
> $1\frac{1}{2}$ cups veal stock (see recipe page 158)
>
> salt and white pepper

Heat the olive oil in a medium sized sauté pan. Add the shallots and cook until they begin to caramelize. Reduce the heat and continue to cook until the shallots are dark brown. Add the veal stock and season with salt and pepper. Keep warm.

## Haricots Verts

$\frac{1}{2}$ pound haricots verts, stem ends removed

2 tablespoons butter

salt and white pepper

Bring a medium-sized pot of water to a boil. Add the haricots verts and cook 3–4 minutes until they are bright green and just tender. Shock the beans in ice water. When ready to serve, reheat the beans in a sauté pan with the butter. Season with salt and pepper.

## Veal Chops

2–3 tablespoons olive oil

6 veal chops (10 ounces each)

salt and black pepper

Preheat the oven to 400F. Heat the oil in a large sauté pan. Season the chops with salt and pepper. When the oil is hot, add the veal chops, be sure not to crowd the pan. You will probably have to sear the chops in 2 or 3 batches. Place the chops on a baking sheet and finish cooking in the oven. The chops should take about 15 minutes to cook. Remove the chops from oven, cover and let rest 10 minutes before serving.

**TO SERVE.** Remove the bread pudding from the molds, and place one in the center of each plate. Arrange the haricots verts to the right. Lean the veal chop on the bread pudding and place the sauce on the bottom $\frac{1}{3}$ of the chop and the front of the plate.

# RED WINE BRAISED VEAL CHEEKS
## *Yukon Gold Potato Pirogi, Wilted Spinach, Carrot Butter Purée*
Serves 4

Make the pirogis a day ahead.

### PIROGI FILLING

> 2 Yukon gold potatoes, peeled and diced
>
> 1 tablespoon olive oil
>
> 2 tablespoons minced shallot
>
> 2 tablespoons crème fraîche (see recipe page 162)
>
> $\frac{1}{2}$ cup grated white cheddar
>
> salt and white pepper

Fill a saucepan with water and bring to a boil. Add the potatoes and cook until tender. Drain the potatoes and process them through a food mill. Heat the olive oil in a small sauté pan over high heat. Add the shallots, cover and sweat them until they are tender. Fold the shallots into the potatoes along with the crème fraîche and the white cheddar. Season with salt and pepper. Place the filling in a pastry bag.

### PIROGI DOUGH

> 6 tablespoons butter
>
> $\frac{1}{2}$ cup milk
>
> 1 egg
>
> $1\frac{1}{2}$ cups flour

Place 4 tablespoons of the butter in a small saucepan over low heat to melt. Cool to room temperature. Place the melted butter, milk, egg and flour in standing mixer with the dough hook attachment. Mix until dough is smooth. Wrap the dough in plastic and let rest for 1 hour.

Divide the dough in half and roll each half into a rectangle. The short end should be the same width as the pasta machine. Start with the widest setting on the pasta machine and roll the dough through. Move the dial to the next setting and roll the dough through. Continue this process until the dough is $\frac{1}{8}$ inch thick. Lay the dough out flat on a table and pipe tablespoons of filling in the center of the pasta sheet, leaving 1 inch between each tablespoon of filling. Lay the second sheet of dough over the filling. Cut a semi-circle with a 3 inch ring mold for each mound of filling. Press the edges to seal. To cook, drop the pirogi into a large pot of boiling water, cook 4–6 minutes. Drain. When ready to serve heat the remaining butter in a large sauté pan, add the pirogi and brown on each side.

*—this recipe continues on the following page*

### WILTED SPINACH

> 2 bunches spinach, washed, dried, and stems removed
>
> 2 tablespoons butter

Bring a large pot of water to a boil. Blanch the spinach 2 minutes, then drain and shock in ice water. When ready to serve, melt the butter in a small sauté pan, add the spinach and heat through.

### CARAMELIZED ONIONS

> 2 tablespoons olive oil
>
> 2 large yellow onions, sliced
>
> 2 tablespoons butter
>
> salt and white pepper

Heat the olive oil in a large sauté pan over high heat. Add the onions and cook until they begin to caramelize. Reduce the heat and continue cooking until the onions have turned mahogany in color. You may need to add a tablespoon of water to deglaze the pan. Just before serving add the butter and season with salt and pepper.

### CARROT BUTTER PURÉE

> 1 tablespoon olive oil
>
> 1 cup diced onion
>
> 3 cups diced carrots
>
> 2 tablespoons butter
>
> salt and white pepper

Heat the olive oil in a sauce pot over high heat. Add the onion, cover and sweat, 4–5 minutes until they are tender. Add the carrots and butter. Cover with water, bring to a boil and simmer until the carrots are tender. Strain, reserving the liquid and the carrots separately. Place the carrot mixture in a food mill and purée. If necessary, add back enough reserved liquid to get to sauce consistency. Strain through a chinois, reheat and season with salt and pepper.

## VEAL CHEEKS

If you can't find veal cheeks you can substitute boneless short ribs.

> 8 veal cheeks
>
> salt and white pepper
>
> 2 tablespoons olive oil
>
> 2 tablespoons minced shallot
>
> 1 cup diced onion
>
> 1 cup diced celery
>
> 1 cup diced carrot
>
> 1 cup red wine
>
> 3 cup beef stock (see recipe page158)
>
> bouquet garni (see page167)

Season the veal cheeks with salt and pepper. Heat 1 tablespoon of the olive oil in a large braising dish. When the oil is hot, sear the cheeks on both sides. Remove from the pot. Add the remaining tablespoon of olive oil, shallots, onion, celery and carrots, cover the pot and sweat the vegetables until they are tender about 10–12 minutes. Uncover the pot, deglaze with the red wine, then add the veal cheeks, beef stock and bouquet garni. Cover, reduce the heat to low and braise for 2 hours until tender. Remove from heat and let rest in the braising liquid for 10 minutes. Remove the veal cheeks from the braising liquid and strain the liquid.

**TO SERVE.** Spoon the carrot purée onto one side of the plate and arrange 3 veal cheeks on top of the purée. Place the spinach on other side of the plate and top it with the pirogi. Top the pirogi with the caramelized onion and spoon braising liquid onto center of the plate.

# VEAL TENDERLOIN MEDALLIONS
*Carnaroli Risotto Arencini, Broccoli Rabe, Truffle Demi-Glace*
Serves 4

The key to good risotto is love and attention. It needs almost constant stirring. Carnaroli is a specific type of rice like Arborio, which has a better quality particularly suited to making risotto.

## RISOTTO

1 tablespoon olive oil

1 tablespoon minced shallots

1 tablespoon minced garlic

1 cup carnaroli rice

$\frac{1}{2}$ cup white wine

2 cups hot white veal stock (see recipe page 158)

2 tablespoons butter

$\frac{1}{2}$ cup grated Parmesan cheese

salt and white pepper

Place the olive oil in a small saucepan over medium high heat. When the oil is hot, add the shallots, garlic and rice. Sauté 3–5 minutes, stirring often. Deglaze with white wine. Continue stirring until the wine has reduced and the pan is dry. Begin adding the veal stock, $\frac{1}{4}$ cup at a time, cooking until the liquid has been absorbed and the rice is tender. Reduce the heat to low, stir in the butter and the cheese and season with salt and pepper.

## BROCCOLI RABE

1 bunch broccoli rabe

2 tablespoons butter

salt and white pepper

Trim the stems from the broccoli rabe and blanch it in boiling water for 2 minutes. Shock in ice water. When ready to serve, reheat with a little butter, salt and pepper.

### TRUFFLE DEMI-GLACE

>   3 cups veal stock (see recipe page 158)

>   3 tablespoons truffle shavings

Place the veal stock in a small sauce pot, bring it to a boil, reduce the heat and simmer until it is reduced by half. Add the truffle shavings.

### VEAL

>   2 tablespoons olive oil

>   2 pounds veal tenderloin

>   salt and black pepper

Preheat the oven to 400°F. Place the olive oil in a large sauté pan over high heat. Season the veal with salt and pepper. When the pan is hot, sear the tenderloin on all sides, then place it in the oven to finish, about 12-15 minutes for medium rare. Remove the veal from oven, cover it and let rest for 15 minutes. Slice the tenderloin on the bias about $\frac{1}{2}$ inch thick.

**TO SERVE.** Place $\frac{1}{2}$ cup of the risotto in a 3 inch ring mold in the center of each plate. Press down lightly with the back of a spoon, then remove. Arrange the broccoli rabe in front of the risotto and lean 3–4 slices of tenderloin on the risotto, covering the ends of the broccoli rabe. Spoon truffle demi-glace on the bottom $\frac{1}{3}$ of the veal and around the plate.

# Black Pepper Grilled Venison Loin
*Potato Fondant, Haricots Verts, Sun-dried Cherry Jus*

Serves 6

## Venison

> 3 pounds venison loin
>
> olive oil
>
> salt and black pepper

Preheat the grill and season the venison with olive oil, cracked black pepper and kosher salt. Place the venison on the grill and sear on all sides. Place over indirect heat and cook to the desired temperature. Remove the venison from the grill, cover and let rest for 10 minutes. When ready to serve slice on the bias $1/2$ inch thick.

## Potato Fondant

> $1^{1}/_{2}$ pounds large Yukon golds potaoes, peeled
>
> 1 tablespoon olive oil
>
> 2 tablespoons minced shallot
>
> 3 tablespoons butter

Cut the potatoes into slabs about $1/2$ inch thick. Using a 3 inch ring mold cut the slabs into circles. Heat the oil in a large pot over medium high heat. Add the shallots, cover and sweat them until tender. Add the potatoes and cover with water. Bring to a boil, reduce the heat and simmer until just tender. Drain and cool. When ready to serve heat the butter in a large sauté pan, add the potatoes and cook them until crisp on both sides. You may need to do it in 2 batches. Keep warm.

## HARICOTS VERTS

    1 pound haricots verts

    1 tablespoon butter

    salt and white pepper

Blanch the haricots verts in a small pot of boiling water for 3–4 minutes, then shock in ice water. When ready to serve, reheat in a sauté pan with the butter. Season with salt and pepper.

## SUN-DRIED CHERRY JUS

    1 cup sundried cherries

    3 cups beef stock (see recipe page 158)

    salt and white pepper

Place the cherries and the beef stock in a small pot and bring to a boil. Reduce the heat and simmer, uncovered, until the liquid is reduced by half. Season with salt and pepper.

TO SERVE. Place a 3 inch ring mold in the center of each plate. Stack the potatoes inside. Remove the ring mold and top with haricots verts. Place the slices of venison in front of the stacked potatoes and drizzle the plate with sun-dried cherry jus.

# Poultry

GRILLED BRICK CHICKEN
*Yukon Gold Panzanella Salad*

2002 Belle Glos "Taylor Lane" Pinot Noir

MAPLE LEAF FARM DUCK CASSOULET
*Ragu of White Beans, Duck Breasts, Roasted Garlic Sausage, Savoy Cabbage*

2000 Chateau Rayas, Chateauneuf-du-Pape

MAPLE LEAF FARM DUCK LEG CONFIT

2002 Knoll "Loibenberg" Riesling Smaragd

MAPLE LEAF FARM DUCK BREAST
*Confit Leg, Warm Potato Croutons, Frisée Salad, Fried Duck Egg*

2002 Panther Creek "Freedom Hill" Pinot Noir

JAPANESE SPICED OSTRICH MEDALLIONS
*Carrot Ginger Purée, Pot Stickers, Sake Reduction*

1999 Pierre Sparr "Mambourg" Gewurztraminer Grand Cru

# GRILLED BRICK CHICKEN
*Yukon Gold Panzanella Salad*
Serves 4

You will need two bricks wrapped in foil for this one or you can buy a grill press at any cooking store.

## CHICKEN

> 2 organic roasting chickens, 3 pounds each, halved and trussed
>
> ¼ cup olive oil
>
> 4 cloves garlic, minced
>
> ¼ cup chiffonade basil leaves
>
> ¼ cup minced parsley
>
> 1 lemon, zested and juiced

Wash and dry the chickens. Place them in a large bowl or ziplock bag. Mix the olive oil, garlic, basil, parsley, lemon zest and juice together, and pour over the chicken. Turn to coat evenly and let marinate 30 minutes.

Preheat the grill. Place the chickens on the grill, bone side down. Place a foil wrapped brick or grill press on top of each chicken. Cook 8–10 minutes, remove the bricks, turn the chickens over and place the bricks back on top. Reduce heat to medium high and cook for another 12–15 minutes or to desired doneness. Remove the chicken from the grill, cover and let rest 10 minutes.

## PANZANELLA SALAD

This is traditionally an Italian Bread salad, but we substituted Yukon gold potatoes for the bread.

> 2 tablespoons butter
>
> 2 pounds cooked Yukon gold potatoes, 1 inch dice
>
> 2 red peppers, roasted, peeled, seeded and julienned (see method page167)
>
> $\frac{1}{4}$ cup capers
>
> $\frac{1}{2}$ cup green olives, pitted
>
> 1 bunch arugula

Melt the butter in a sauté pan. Add the potatoes and brown on all sides. Place them in a large bowl with the julienned peppers, capers and green olives. When ready to serve, add the arugula and dressing to the potato mixture. Toss to coat evenly.

## DRESSING

> 1 tablespoon minced shallot
>
> 1 large lemon, juiced and zested
>
> $\frac{1}{4}$ cup olive oil
>
> salt and white pepper
>
> basil oil (see recipe page 163)

Place shallots, lemon juice, zest and olive oil in a small bowl, and whisk to combine. Season to taste with salt and pepper.

TO SERVE. Place about a cup of the panzanella salad in the center of each plate. Then top with half of a chicken and drizzle with basil oil.

# MAPLE LEAF FARM DUCK CASSOULET

*Ragu of White Beans, Duck Breast, Roasted Garlic Sausage, Savoy Cabbage*

Serves 8

## WHITE BEANS

$1\frac{1}{2}$ cups white beans, soaked in water overnight

1 tablespoon olive oil

$\frac{1}{2}$ cup diced onion

$\frac{1}{2}$ cup diced celery

$\frac{1}{2}$ cup diced carrot

2 cloves garlic, minced

1 shallot, minced

2 cups duck stock (see recipe page 159)

1 tablespoon minced thyme

1 tablespoon minced rosemary

1 bay leaf

Drain the beans, then place them in a small pot and cover with water. Bring to a boil then drain. Heat the olive oil in large stock pot over high heat. Add the onion, celery, carrots, garlic and shallots and sauté 2–3 minutes. Reduce the heat, cover and sweat the vegetables for 10 minutes. Add the beans, duck stock, thyme, rosemary and bay leaf. Bring to a boil, reduce the heat, cover and simmer 2–3 hours or until the beans are tender. You may need to add water occasionally to keep the beans covered, but don't add too much. You want the liquid in the beans to have the consistency of gravy when they are finished cooking.

## ROASTED GARLIC SAUSAGE

1 tablespoon olive oil

$\frac{1}{2}$ cup diced onion

2 pounds raw duck meat, cubed

$\frac{3}{4}$ pound pork fat, cubed

4 cloves garlic, minced

$\frac{1}{4}$ cup minced parsley

1 tablespoon salt

$\frac{1}{2}$ tablespoon white pepper

$\frac{1}{4}$ teaspoon ground sage

$\frac{1}{4}$ teaspoon ground coriander

Heat the olive oil in a small sauté pan. When the oil is hot, add the onion, cover and sweat until tender and translucent. Cool. Force the duck meat and pork fat through a meat grinder. Place them in a small bowl with all other ingredients and mix until combined evenly. Stuff the sausage meat into casings. Bring a large pot of water to a boil. Reduce the heat to simmer and poach the sausages until they are cooked, about 12–15 minutes. Remove the sausages from the water and cool. Preheat grill. When ready to serve, place the sausages on the grill to brown on all sides.

### DUCK BREASTS

> 8 duck breasts
>
> salt and black pepper
>
> 1 tablespoon olive oil

Season the duck breasts with salt and pepper. Place the olive oil in a large sauté pan over medium high heat. Add the duck, breast skin side down and cook the skin until it is golden and very crisp, about 10 minutes. Flip over and cook the flesh side for about 2 minutes. Remove the duck from the pan. Cover and let the duck rest 3–5 minutes before serving. Then slice on the bias.

### CABBAGE

> 2 tablespoons butter
>
> $\frac{1}{2}$ head savoy cabbage, thinly sliced

Melt the butter in a small sauté pan. Add the cabbage and cook until the cabbage is just wilted.

> 8 confit duck legs (see recipe next page)
>
> microgreens

TO SERVE. Fill a 3 inch ring mold with the white beans in the center of the serving plate, press the beans down with the back of a spoon and remove the mold. Cover the front $\frac{1}{3}$ of plate with cabbage. Lean the duck legs on the side of the beans and fan out the breast on top of the cabbage in the front of the plate. Place the sausage on the left side of the plate and garnish with microgreens.

# MAPLE LEAF FARM DUCK LEG CONFIT

You can buy rendered duck fat on line at clubsauce.com

> 1 pound kosher salt
>
> 1 pound sugar
>
> $\frac{1}{2}$ cup juniper berries
>
> 6 duck legs
>
> 12 sprigs thyme
>
> 12–14 cups WARM duck fat

Mix the salt and sugar together in a small bowl. Grind the juniper berries in a spice grinder. Place the duck legs on a large piece of cheesecloth on a wire rack. Place two of the thyme sprigs on each leg. Coat each leg with the crushed juniper berries and the salt/sugar mixture. Wrap the cheesecloth around the legs. Place the duck on a wire rack inside a roasting pan and refrigerate for 12 hours. Remove the duck legs from the refrigerator, rinse with cold water, and pat dry. Let air dry for 1 hour.

Preheat the oven to 180°F. Place the legs in a roasting pan large enough to fit the legs without crowding. Pour the warm duck fat over the legs, making sure they are completely submerged. Place the pan in the oven and roast for 5 hours until the duck is very tender. Let the duck cool in the fat. The legs will keep this way for 2 weeks.

When ready to serve, reheat the legs in the fat in a low oven until the fat is melted. Remove the legs carefully from the pan and place in a very hot cast iron skillet, (or heavy sauté pan), containing 2–3 tablespoons of the melted duck fat. Place the legs in the pan skin side down and heat for 8–12 minutes until crispy. Let them rest 2–3 minutes until serving.

# MAPLE LEAF FARM DUCK BREAST
## *Confit Leg, Warm Potato Croutons, Frisée Salad, Fried Duck Egg*
### Serves 6

You can buy duck eggs at your local farmers market or online at duckeggs.com.

## CROUTONS

3 squares butternut squash and potato gratin (see recipe page 104)

1/2 cup flour

2 eggs, beaten

1 cup Japanese bread crumbs (panko)

3 tablespoons butter

6 duck eggs

Preheat the deep fryer to 375°F. Cut the potato gratin into 24 cubes (1 inch). Place the flour, eggs and panko into 3 separate bowls. Dip the cubes into flour, then eggs, then panko. Fry the "croutons" in oil in several batches, 3–5 minutes until golden, drain.

## FRISÉE

3 heads frisée

1 tablespoon red wine vinegar

3 tablespoons olive oil

salt and white pepper

Cut the frisée heads in half and place them in a bowl. Add the red wine vinegar, olive oil, salt and pepper. Toss to coat.

## DUCK EGGS

3 tablespoons butter

6 duck eggs

Melt butter in a large non stick pan over medium high heat. Add the duck eggs, reduce heat to medium and cook until the bottoms are set about 3 minutes (you may want to do this in 2 pans).

## DUCK BREASTS

salt and black pepper

6 duck breasts

Season the duck breasts with salt and pepper. Place the breasts in a large sauté pan skin side down over medium high heat. Render the skin until it is golden and very crisp (about 10 minutes). Flip over the duck and cook on flesh side for about 2 minutes. Remove from the pan heat. Let rest 3–5 minutes before serving. Then slice on the bias.

6 confit duck legs (see recipe page 123)

TO SERVE. Place 1/2 head frisee in the center of each plate. Lean the duck leg on the frisée and place the sliced duck breast in front of the plate. Garnish with the croutons and duck egg.

# JAPANESE SPICED OSTRICH MEDALLIONS
*Carrot Ginger Purée, Pot Stickers, Sake Reduction*
Serves 6

You can find ostrich in some specialty grocery stores or online at eprimecuts.com
If you can't find ostrich you can substitute venison. You will have left over pot stickers, freeze them and serve as an appetizer.

## POT STICKERS

> 2 tablespoons olive oil
>
> 1 tablespoon minced garlic
>
> 1 tablespoon minced ginger
>
> ½ bunch scallions, minced
>
> 8 ounces ground pork
>
> salt and white pepper
>
> 1 egg, beaten with 1 teaspoon water
>
> 50 wonton skins (1 package)

Heat 1 tablespoon of the olive oil in a sauté pan. Add the garlic, ginger and scallions and sauté 2 minutes. Add the pork, reduce the heat and cook through. Add the salt and pepper to taste. Cool. Place one wonton wrapper on a flat work surface. Dip a pastry brush into the egg wash and brush the edges of the wonton wrapper. Place one teaspoon of the filling in center of the wrapper. (You may need to break up large lumps of meat with your fingers or mince.) Fold the wrapper in half and seal the edges. Be sure to press all the air out of the inside. Fold, crimp, or pleat the edges. You can freeze them at this point. When ready to serve, heat the remaining tablespoon of olive oil in a large sauté pan. Add half of the pot stickers and sear on one side. (You may need to do this in 2 or 3 batches so the pan does not get overcrowded.) When brown, turn the pot stickers over, add the sake reduction and cook 2 minutes more.

## CARROT GINGER PURÉE

> 5 carrots, peeled and diced
>
> 1 tablespoon minced ginger

Place the carrots and ginger in a small saucepot. Cover the carrots with water, bring to a boil, reduce to a simmer and cook until the carrots are very tender. Drain. Place the carrots in a food mill and purée. Reheat with a little butter and form into quenelles. To form a quenelle, use 2 spoons and shape into a small oval.

## Sake Reduction

Sake is Japanese rice wine.

> 2 cups sake
>
> 2 cups tomato juice
>
> 2 tablespoons butter

Place sake and tomato juice in small saucepot. Bring to a boil, reduce the heat and simmer until the liquid has reduced by half. Whisk in the butter.

## Ostrich

You can buy Japanese Seven Spice (Shichimi Togarashi) premixed in the spice section of Asian grocery stores. It consists of red chile flakes, sansho (Szechuan pepper), white sesame seeds, nori and bits of dried mandarin orange peel, hemp seeds and white poppy seeds. It is available in hot, medium and mild.

> 3 pounds ostrich strip loin
>
> 3 tablespoons Japanese Seven Spice
>
> 2 tablespoons olive oil

Rub the ostrich sparingly with Japanese Seven spice. Heat the oil in a large sauté pan over medium high heat. Place the ostrich in the pan and sear on all sides. Ostrich is a very lean meat, so we recommend you don't cook it more than medium rare or it will be dry and tough. Cover, let rest 10 minutes, then slice on the bias $1/4$ inch thick.

**TO SERVE.** Place 4 carrot quenelles in the center of the plate, tips together. Arrange 4 pot stickers between the carrot quenelles. Arrange 5 ostrich medallions around the outside of the plate. Spoon about 2 ounces ($1/4$ cup) sake reduction around plate.

128

# — PASTA

### ENGLISH PEA AGNOLOTTI
*Morels and Pea Shoots, Périgord Truffle*

2000 Jean-Marc Brocard "Les Clos" Chablis Grand Cru

### FOIE GRAS RAVIOLI
*Lobster Buerre Fondu*

1996 Pol Roget Brut Rose Champagne

### TAGLIARINI
*Truffles, Reggiano, Duck Egg*

2001 Conterno Fantino "Vignota" Barbera

### ROASTED SQUASH TORTELLINI
*Cauliflower Florets, Walnut Brown Butter, Marjoram*

2002 Planeta Winery Chardonnay, Sicily

# ENGLISH PEA AGNOLOTTI
*Morels and Pea Shoots, Périgord Truffles*
Serves 8

In Italian agnolotti means, "priests' caps". They are small, stuffed, delicate pillows of dough that are actually quite easy to make.

## AGNOLOTTI FILLING

    4 cups shucked English peas

    $\frac{1}{2}$ cup finely grated Parmesan cheese

    salt and white pepper

Bring a large pot of water to a boil. Add the peas and blanch 5 minutes, drain. Place the warm peas in a food mill and purée. Stir in the Parmesan cheese and season with salt and pepper. Place the filling in a pastry bag.

    pasta dough (see recipe on page 165)

Divide the dough in half and roll it out into a rectangle. The short end should be the same width as the pasta machine. Start with the widest setting and roll the dough through. Move the dial to the next setting and roll the dough through. Continue this process until the dough is $\frac{1}{8}$ inch thick. Pipe tablespoons of filling the length of each pasta sheet leaving a $\frac{1}{2}$ inch edge along the bottom. Fold the bottom edge over the filling and then press down to seal. Run a pastry wheel along the sealed edge. Starting at one end of the dough, pinch the filling into pillows about 1 inch wide. Then run the pastry wheel through the center of each pinch. You will get about 12 pillows per sheet of dough. Place the pasta on a parchment lined baking sheet and freeze until ready to use. (See photos on how to make agnolotti on page 136.)

*—this recipe continues on the following page*

## MORELS AND PEA SHOOTS

Dau Miu is Cantonese for "pea shoots". They are available in Chinese markets in the spring.

> 1 tablespoon olive oil
>
> 2 tablespoons minced shallot
>
> 24 morels
>
> $\frac{1}{2}$ pound pea shoots
>
> $\frac{1}{4}$ cup white wine
>
> $1\frac{1}{2}$ cups heavy cream
>
> salt and white pepper
>
> truffle oil

Heat the olive oil in a large sauté pan over medium high heat. Add the shallots, cover and sweat 2–3 minutes. Add the morels and pea shoots, sauté for 3 minutes then deglaze with white wine. Add the cream and let it reduce by half. Season with salt and pepper.

TO SERVE. Bring a large pot of salted water to a boil. Add half of the pasta and cook it 5–8 minutes until it is tender. Remove the pasta from the water with a slotted spoon or spider. Repeat with the second half. Place 10–12 pieces in each of 8 serving bowls. Spoon 3 morels into each bowl, place a few pea shoots on top of the pasta and spoon some of the sauce over the top. Drizzle with truffle oil.

# FOIE GRAS RAVIOLI
*Lobster Buerre Fondu*
### Serves 4

If you don't have time to cure a lobe of foie gras yourself, you can buy a cured medallion on line at deananddeluca.com It is important that you use good sea salt here. Fleur de sel, or flower of salt, is salt harvested from the coast of France. The crystals are longer and have a more intense flavor.

## FOIE GRAS

> 6 ounce lobe foie gras
>
> $^1/_2$ cup sauternes
>
> 1 teaspoon fleur de sel

Remove any visible veins from the foie gras. Cut it into small cubes and place in a small flat glass dish. Toss the foie gras with the sauternes and salt to coat it evenly. Cover and let marinate 2 hours. Drain it in a chinois, rinse with cold water and pat dry.

## RAVIOLI

> pasta dough (see recipe page 165)
>
> 6 ounces cured foie gras
>
> 1 egg beaten with 1 tablespoon water

Divide the dough in half and roll it out into a rectangle. The short end should be the same width as the pasta machine. Start with the widest setting and roll the dough through. Move the dial to the next setting and roll the dough through. Continue this process until the dough is $^1/_8$ inch thick. Cut the sheets into 2 inch squares. Place a tablespoon of foie gras in the center of 12 squares. Lightly egg-wash the outside edges of the pasta squares. Place another square of pasta on top and press lightly to seal edges. (You may freeze or refrigerate them at this point.)

When ready to serve, bring a large pot of water to a boil. Add the ravioli and cook 2–3 minutes, then gently remove them from water with a slotted spoon or spider.

LOBSTER

> $1\frac{1}{4}$ pound lobster
>
> 1 pound butter, clarified (see recipe page 162)

(If you are squeamish about killing the lobster yourself, when you buy it ask them to separate the tail, claws and body for you. If not, see instructions on how to kill a lobster on page 7)

Kill the lobster and remove the tail and claws. Warm the butter in a small pot over medium heat and add the tail. Poach 10 minutes. Remove the tail and add the claws. Poach 8 minutes. Remove the claws and add the body. Poach 10 minutes. Reserve separately the tail, claws and the butter. Discard the lobster body. Remove the meat from the tail and slice it into 8 pieces. Remove the meat from the claws and cut them into 8 pieces. Refrigerate the butter until it solidifies.

BUERRE FONDU

> buerre blanc (see recipe page 162)

Make buerre blanc according to the recipe, except substitute the lobster butter for regular butter.

TO SERVE. Place 3 ravioli in each of 4 serving bowls. Divide the reserved lobster meat evenly among the serving bowls, spoon a little lobster buerre fondu over the ravioli and serve immediately.

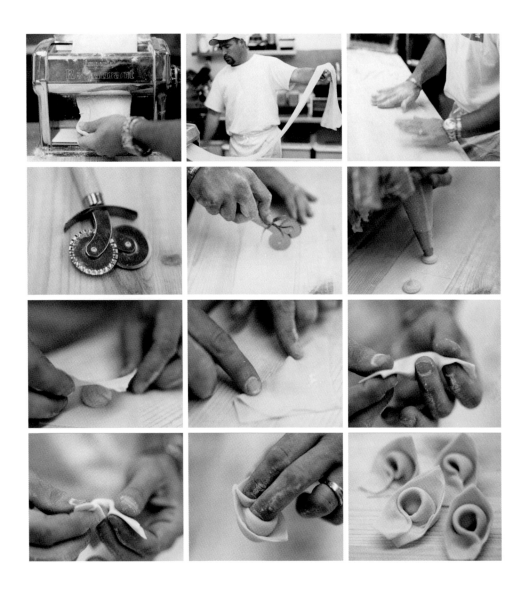

# Tagliarini
*Truffles, Reggiano, Duck Egg*
Serves 4

The decadent simplicity of this dish is what makes it so delicious. You can find truffle peelings on line at deananddeluca.com or where gourmet groceries are available.

>   pasta dough (see recipe page 165)

Divide the dough in half and roll it out into a rectangle. The short end should be the same width as the pasta machine. Start with the widest setting and roll the dough through. Move the dial to the next setting and roll the dough through. Continue this process until the dough is $\frac{1}{8}$ inch thick. Lay the pasta sheet flat on a work surface and cut it into strips $\frac{1}{8}$-inch wide. You may want to use a yardstick to keep your cuts even. If you have an attachment to cut thin strips or a pasta bike to cut the strips it will make it easier. You can dry the strips on a rack or cook immediately.

>   $\frac{1}{4}$ cup white truffle oil
>
>   $\frac{1}{4}$ cup melted European style butter, such as Plugra

Place a large pot of water over high heat and bring to a boil. Add the pasta to the pot and cook 3 minutes until tender. Drain and then toss with the truffle oil and butter.

>   2 tablespoons butter
>
>   4 duck eggs

Place a small sauté pan over high heat and add the butter. When melted, add the eggs, reduce the heat to medium-low and cook until the whites are set, 3–4 minutes.

>   Parmigiano Reggiano
>
>   truffle peelings

TO SERVE. Divide the pasta among 4 serving bowls. Top each with a duck egg, sunny side up. Shave Parmesan on the top. Then top with truffle peelings.

# ROASTED SQUASH TORTELLINI
*Cauliflower Florets, Walnut Brown Butter, Marjoram*
Serves 4

## SQUASH FILLING

> 1 large butternut squash
>
> 2 tablespoons butter
>
> 2 teaspoons brown sugar
>
> 2 teaspoons fresh lemon juice
>
> 1 cup finely grated Parmesan cheese
>
> nutmeg
>
> Amaretti cookie
>
> salt and white pepper

Preheat the oven to 350°F. Cut the squash in half, remove the seeds, and place both halves on a sheet tray, flesh side up. Divide the butter, brown sugar and lemon juice between the halves. Season each with salt and pepper. Place the squash in the oven and cook until very tender, about 60 minutes. Remove it from the oven, let cool slightly, then scoop out the squash flesh with a spoon. Purée the squash using a food mill. Add the Parmesan cheese and then grate a little nutmeg and Amaretti cookie into the squash. Season with salt and pepper. Place the filling in a pastry bag.

> 1 recipe pasta dough (see recipe page 165)

Divide the dough in half and roll it out into a rectangle. The short end should be the same width as the pasta machine. Start with the widest setting and roll the dough through. Move the dial to the next setting and roll the dough through. Continue this process until the dough is $\frac{1}{8}$ inch thick. Cut the sheets into 2 inch squares and pipe about a tablespoon of the filling into the center of each square. Moisten the edges lightly with water then fold the pasta square in half over the filling to make a triangle. Place your index finger in the center back of the triangle and pull the opposite ends around your finger to create the tortellini shape. Place the tortellini on a parchment lined baking sheet and freeze until ready to use. (See photos on how to make tortellini on page 137.)

TO SERVE. Heat a large pot of water over high heat. When it comes to a boil, add the tortellini and boil about 3 minutes until tender. Remove the pasta with a slotted spoon or spider and divide it among 4 serving bowls.

$\frac{1}{2}$ cup walnuts, toasted  (to toast nuts, see recipe page 167)

1 stick of butter, browned  (to brown butter, see recipe page 153)

$\frac{1}{2}$ head cauliflower, florets only, blanched

4 tablespoons marjoram, minced, plus more for garnish

Heat the walnuts, butter, cauliflower florets and marjoram in a small sauté pan. Divide the mixture among the pasta bowls and garnish with marjoram.

## Desserts

PEAR BREAD PUDDING
*Ginger-Pear Ice Cream, Caramel Sauce*

WARM MILK CHOCOLATE CAKE
*Grand Marnier Ice Cream*

PALISADE PEACH CROSTADA
*Peach Ice Cream, White Chocolate Sauce*

COLORADO CHERRY CLAFOUTI
*Chocolate Sauce, Whipped Cream*

PHILLIPPE'S HAZELNUT GÂTEAU
*Vanilla Ice Cream, Caramel Sauce*

# PEAR BREAD PUDDING
*Ginger-Pear Ice Cream, Caramel Sauce*
Serves 9

## BREAD PUDDING

6 eggs, beaten

1 cup milk

1 cup heavy cream

3 pears, peeled, cored and diced

1 teaspoon cinnamon

1 cup dried cherries

1 loaf brioche, cubed and dried (see recipe page 165 )

Butter a square (9x9x2) baking dish. Preheat the oven to 350°F. In a small bowl whisk together the eggs, milk, cream, pears, cinnamon and cherries. Add the broiche cubes and toss, coating them well. Pour the entire mixture into the prepared baking dish and place in oven for 1 hour, until it is set. Remove the pudding from the oven and let rest 15 minutes. Cut into squares.

## GINGER-PEAR ICE CREAM

3 ripe pears

4 egg yolks

$\frac{1}{2}$ cup brown sugar

1 cup milk

1 cup heavy cream

2 tablespoons minced ginger

Peel and core the pears, then purée them in a food processor. Whisk the egg yolks and sugar together in a small bowl until the sugar dissolves. Put the milk and cream in a medium sauce pan and bring to a simmer over medium heat. When the milk mixture is hot, pour half of it into egg yolks and stir to temper. Pour back into the saucepan and cook until thickened. Strain the mixture through a chinois, add the pear puré and ginger, then chill in the refrigerator. When it is cold, freeze the mixture in an ice cream maker according to manufacturer's instructions.

## CARAMEL SAUCE (see recipe page 154)

**TO SERVE.** For each serving, cut a square of warm bread pudding in half diagonally making two triangles. Place the warm triangles (one on its side) on a plate and top with the ice cream and caramel sauce.

# WARM MILK CHOCOLATE CAKE
## *Grand Marnier Ice Cream*
Serves 6

These cakes should be liquid chocolate in the center. Don't over bake them.

### CAKE

4 ounces butter

4 ounces bittersweet chocolate

4 ounces milk chocolate

2 whole eggs

3 egg yolks

1 cups cake flour

$\frac{3}{4}$ cup powdered sugar

Preheat the oven to 350°F. Butter 6 (6 ounce) ramekins. Place the butter and the chocolate together in a small bowl and place bowl over a pot of simmering water until melted.

Place the whole eggs and egg yolks in the bowl of a standing mixer. Whip until the eggs are double in volume. With the mixer running, slowly add the butter mixture in a thin stream. Sift the flour and sugar together, then carefully fold into the chocolate mixture by hand. Divide the batter equally among the buttered ramekins and bake until set, 15–20 minutes.

### GRAND MARNIER ICE CREAM

4 egg yolks

$\frac{1}{2}$ cup sugar

1 cup milk

1 cup heavy cream

$\frac{1}{4}$ cup Grand Marnier

Whip the egg yolks and sugar in a small bowl until the sugar dissolves. Place the milk, cream and Grand Marnier together in a small sauce pan. Bring to a boil, turn off the heat and let it cool slightly. Temper half of the milk mixture into the egg yolks. Pour the entire mixture back into the pan and stir on low heat until thickened. Strain the mixture through a fine mesh chinois, and then refrigerate until cold. Freeze in an ice cream maker according to manufacturer's recommendations.

### CHOCOLATE SAUCE

8 ounces bittersweet chocolate, chopped

1 cup heavy cream

Place the chocolate and cream in a sauce pan over medium low heat and stir until the chocolate melts. Cool to room temperature and pour into a squeeze tube.

**TO SERVE.** Warm the cakes and invert onto dessert plates. Top with a scoop of ice cream. Drizzle plate with chocolate sauce.

# PALISADE PEACH CROSTADA
*Peach Ice Cream, White Chocolate Sauce*
### Serves 8

Palisade, Colorado is known for growing great peaches; they are available in August and September.

## PÂTE SUCRÉE

>3 cups flour
>
>$\frac{1}{2}$ cup sugar
>
>$\frac{1}{4}$ teaspoon salt
>
>2 sticks butter, diced
>
>2 eggs

Place the flour, sugar and salt in the bowl of a standing mixer or food processor. Add the butter one cube at time until all the butter is incorporated and the mixture resembles fine cornmeal. Add the eggs one at a time and mix until a smooth dough forms. Split the dough in half, form into small discs and wrap in plastic wrap. Refrigerate for at least 2 hours or overnight.

Preheat the oven to 375°F. Remove one piece of dough from refrigerator and let it warm up for 10 minutes. Roll out the dough into a 12 inch circle (it should be about $\frac{1}{4}$ inch thick). Transfer the dough to a 10 inch tart pan with a removable bottom. Cut the dough to within $\frac{1}{2}$ inch of the edge of tart pan. Fold the edge of the dough back over itself into the pan to form a double thick fluted edge. Line the tart shell with foil and fill with pie weights or dried beans. Bake the tart shell for 40 minutes until almost set. Remove pie weights and bake 10 minutes more, then cool to room temperature.

## FILLING

>$1\frac{1}{2}$ pounds Palisade peaches
>
>$\frac{1}{4}$ teaspoon cinnamon
>
>$\frac{1}{4}$ teaspoon nutmeg
>
>2 whole cloves
>
>$\frac{1}{4}$ cup brown sugar
>
>1 cup peach jam
>
>1 tablespoon fresh lemon juice
>
>1 egg beaten with 1 tablespoon water

Bring a large pot of water to a boil. Cut an x in the bottom of each peach. Gently place the peaches in the boiling water for 1 minute. Remove them from the pot and place in ice water. Peel the peaches and then slice them into $\frac{1}{4}$ inch thick pieces. Place 1 pound of the sliced peaches, the cinnamon, nutmeg, cloves and brown sugar in a bowl and let marinate for 1 hour, while the tart shell bakes. Strain the liquid from the peaches and reserve. Mix the peach jam with the lemon juice. Spread it in an even layer over bottom of the tart shell. Arrange the peaches in an even layer on top of the jam in concentric circles. Remove the second piece of dough from refrigerator. Let it warm for 10 minutes and then roll as the first piece. Using a fluted pastry wheel, cut 1 inch wide strips of dough. Place strips of dough across tart shell to create a lattice crust. First lay a strip horizontally across the tart and then lay the next strip across the tart vertically crossing the first strip at the top left. The third strip should be horizontal crossing the second strip in the top left and so on, work your way down the tart until it is covered. Trim off any overhanging strips. There should be 4–5 vertical and 4–5 horizontal strips. Dip a pastry brush in the egg wash and coat the top crust and edges. Place the tart in the oven and bake it for another 45 minutes until the crust is golden. Let it cool in the tart pan. Remove the tart from pan when ready to serve. Cut into 8 pieces.

## WHITE CHOCOLATE SAUCE

> 6 ounces white chocolate, chopped
>
> $3/4$ cup heavy cream

Combine the chocolate and cream in a small sauce pan over medium heat. Stir until the chocolate melts, strain. Pour the mixture into a squeeze tube and cool to room temperature.

## PEACH ICE CREAM

> Reserved $1/2$ pound sliced peaches
>
> Reserved peach marinade, from filling recipe
>
> 4 egg yolks
>
> $1/2$ cup sugar
>
> 1 cup milk
>
> 1 cup heavy cream
>
> 1 teaspoon vanilla

Place the reserved peaches in a blender with the reserved peach marinade. Purée until smooth. Combine the egg yolks and sugar and stir until sugar is dissolved. Place the milk and cream in a small sauce pan and bring to a simmer. Whisk about half into the eggs yolks to temper, then pour all of it back into the sauce pan, and stir until thickened. Add the vanilla and peach purée, stir to combine. Strain through a chinois and refrigerate until cold. Pour the cold mixture into an ice cream maker and freeze according to manufacturer's recommendations.

TO SERVE. Place one slice of warm crostada on each dessert plate, top with one scoop of the ice cream and drizzle with white chocolate sauce.

# COLORADO CHERRY CLAFOUTI
*Chocolate Sauce, Whipped Cream*
Serves 8

The Western Slope of Colorado is known for growing great fruit. We try to use as many of them as we can.

## CLAFOUTI

1 pound Colorado Bing cherries, plus a few for garnish

3 eggs

½ cup sugar

4 tablespoons butter, melted

⅔ cup flour

⅔ cup milk

confectioner's sugar

Preheat the oven to 400°F. Butter an 8 inch fluted pie dish. Cut the cherries in half and remove the pits. Place them flat side down in pie dish in an even layer. Place the eggs in the bowl of an electric mixer and beat on low speed with the whisk attachment until they are pale yellow in color. With mixer still running, add the sugar in a thin stream, then beat 1 minute more. Do the same with the melted butter. Add the flour all at once and mix briefly, just to combine. Add the milk in a thin stream and whisk until smooth. Gently pour the batter over the cherries, being careful not to disturb them. Place the dish in the oven and bake for 30–40 minutes until set. Let cool, then sprinkle with powdered sugar. Cut into 8 pieces.

## CHOCOLATE SAUCE (see recipe page 146)

## WHIPPED CREAM

1 cup heavy cream

3 tablespoons powdered sugar

1 teaspoon vanilla

Place all of the ingredients in a bowl and whisk until thickened. Do not over mix.

## GARNISH

sprigs of mint

TO SERVE. Drizzle each plate with chocolate sauce. Place one slice of clafouti on each dessert plate, on its side. Garnish with a dollop of whipped cream, a couple of cherries and a sprig of mint.

# PHILLIPPE'S HAZELNUT GÂTEAU
*Vanilla Ice Cream, Caramel Sauce*
Serves 8

If you can't find hazelnut or almond flour, toast the nuts and grind them to a fine crumb in your food processor. Nutella is a name brand for hazelnut spread, it is similar to peanut butter.

## GÂTEAU

1½ sticks butter

7 egg whites

½ cup plus 2 tablespoons sugar

1 cup hazelnut flour

½ cup almond flour

2 tablespoons honey

8 teaspoons nutella

Preheat the oven to 300°F. Spray 8 (6 ounce) ramekins with non stick cooking spray. Heat the butter over high heat until it has melted. Reduce the heat to medium and continue cooking until the butter browns. Cool to room temperature.

Place the egg whites in the bowl of an electric mixer. Whip them to the soft peak stage. With the mixer running, add the brown butter in a thin stream until it is fully incorporated. You may need to stop and scrape down the sides of the bowl periodically. Slowly add the sugar, then the flours and honey. Pour the mixture into ramekins, filling them ¾ full. Place the ramekins on a baking sheet and place in the oven. Bake 30–40 minutes. Test for doneness by touching the center of the cake. If it stays indented, bake a few more minutes until the cake springs back. Let the cakes cool. Remove center of each cake by scoring it with a 1 inch ring mold, then pull the center out and reserve. Fill the center with nutella then place the center cake piece back in.

*—this recipe continues on the following page*

## VANILLA ICE CREAM

    4 egg yolks

    ½ cup sugar

    1 vanilla bean

    1 cup milk

    1 cup heavy cream

Whisk the egg yolks together with the sugar in a small bowl until the sugar dissolves. Place the milk and cream in a small sauce pan. Split the vanilla bean and scrape it into the pan. Bring it to a simmer. Whisk half of the hot cream into the egg yolks to temper them. Then whisk the tempered egg yolks back into the pan. Place the pan over medium low heat and stir until thickened. Strain the mixture through a chinois and refrigerate until cold. When cold, freeze in ice cream maker according to the manufacturer's recommendations.

## CARAMEL SAUCE

    1 cup sugar

    ¼ cup water

    2 tablespoon butter

    ½ cup heavy cream

Place the sugar in the center of a very clean heavy bottomed sauce pan (Copper works best). Add the water and turn on low heat. Leave undisturbed until the sugar has dissolved and started to turn golden brown. Remove from the heat, then slowly add the butter and cream, stir with a wooden spoon until smooth. It will bubble up.

## GARNISH

    24 hazelnuts, toasted (see recipe page 167)

    1–2 tablespoons cocoa powder

    mint sprigs

Place the hazelnuts in a small bowl and toss with the cocoa powder to coat.

TO SERVE. Warm the cakes in the oven, invert on dessert plates and remove the ramekins. Drizzle the plates with caramel sauce and top with vanilla ice cream. Garnish with cocoa covered hazelnuts and a mint sprig.

# BASICS

STOCK

BUTTER, OIL AND CREAM

DOUGH

MISCELLANEOUS

COOKING TERMS AND EQUIPMENT

### A LITTLE NOTE FROM JILL

WHEN FRANK CALLED ME and asked me to help him write a book, I was very intrigued. I had known of him for a long time and had his cooking many times over the years, but I had never had the pleasure of working with him in the kitchen. So before I started writing, I asked to work in the kitchen for a few nights to learn Mizuna's philosophy and style of cooking. One of the first things the chefs told me was "garbage in - garbage out" meaning, if you don't start with the best ingredients, you are not going to get the best finished product. There are a few other important things to know before you cook any of these recipes. Be very meticulous about cutting everything the same size, so it all cooks in the same amount of time. You can cook a 1" diced potato much faster than you can cook a 2" diced potato. It is also very important to truss the meat you are cooking, so it is uniform in size and cooks evenly. After cooking always allow meat to rest at least ten minutes before you serve it. Mizuna changes the menu every month, so they stay in tune with what is freshest and what is locally available. They are proud of the amount of Colorado grown produce and meat on their menu. Other tips: use kosher salt, freshly ground pepper (they prefer white pepper for most items, it is milder than black pepper and does not taint the color of the food), really good extra virgin olive oil and European style butter. If a recipe calls for wine, use a good quality wine that you like and that goes with the dish. Bring this cookbook out if you are treating yourself, it is the anti-diet cookbook, forsaking all trends for a great tasting indulgence.

# STOCK

Good stock is a very important part of any dish. It is important to use the same stock as the meat you are preparing. The most important thing to remember is to ALWAYS start with cold water.

## BEEF, VEAL, LAMB OR PORK STOCK

> 5 pounds bones
>
> 2 yellow onions, diced
>
> 2 leeks, sliced
>
> 4 ribs celery, diced
>
> 2 carrots, diced
>
> 4 tablespoons tomato paste
>
> $\frac{1}{2}$ cup red wine
>
> 2 bay leaves
>
> 1 tablespoon peppercorns

Preheat the oven to 375°F. Place the bones in a large baking dish and roast for 1 hour turning once or twice until evenly browned on all sides. Combine the onions, leeks, celery, carrots and tomato paste in a bowl and stir to coat vegetables evenly. Add the mixture to the bones and roast another 30–45 minutes until browned. Deglaze the roasting pan with red wine, be sure to scrape all the brown bits from the pan.

Transfer the contents of the roasting pan to a large stock pot and place on the stove over high heat. Add enough cold water to cover the bones, and let it come to a boil. Reduce heat and simmer 8 hours. Periodically skim the foam from the top. Strain and reserve the bone mixture and stock separately. Again cover the bones with cold water, bring to a boil, reduce heat and simmer 8 hours. Strain, discard the bones and vegetables. Combine the 2 stocks and reduce by two-thirds. To make demi-glace, continue to reduce stock by half.

## WHITE BEEF, VEAL, LAMB OR PORK STOCK

> 5 pounds bones
>
> 2 yellow onions, diced
>
> 2 leeks, sliced
>
> 4 ribs celery, diced
>
> 2 carrots, diced
>
> 2 bay leaves
>
> 1 tablespoon peppercorns

Combine all of the ingredients in a large stock pot. Cover with cold water and bring to a boil, reduce heat and simmer 8 hours. Periodically skim the foam from the top. Strain and reserve bone mixture and stock separately. Again cover the bones with cold water, bring to a boil, reduce heat and simmer 8 hours. Strain, discard the bones and vegetables. Combine the 2 stocks and reduce by two-thirds.

## CHICKEN OR DUCK STOCK

5 pounds chicken or duck bones

2 yellow onions, diced

2 leeks, sliced

4 ribs celery, diced

2 carrots, diced

4 tablespoons tomato paste

$\frac{1}{4}$ cup red wine

2 bay leaves

1 tablespoon peppercorns

Preheat the oven to 375°F. Place the bones in a large baking dish and roast for 1 hour until evenly browned on all sides. Combine the onions, leeks, celery, carrots and tomato paste in a bowl and stir to coat vegetables evenly. Add the mixture to the bones and roast another 30–45 minutes until browned. Deglaze the roasting pan with red wine, be sure to scrape all the brown bits from the pan. Transfer the contents of the roasting pan to a large stock pot and place on the stove over a high heat. Add enough cold water to cover the bones and let it come to a boil. Reduce the heat and simmer 4 hours. Strain and reserve the bone mixture and stock separately. Again cover the bones with cold water, bring to a boil, reduce heat and simmer 4 hours. Periodically skim the foam from the top. Strain, discarding the bones and vegetables. Combine the 2 stocks and reduce by two-thirds.

Note: If you want a clear chicken or duck stock, skip the roasting of the bones and vegetables, just put them all in the stock pot and cover with cold water. Bring to a boil, reduce the heat and simmer 4 hours. Strain and reserve the stock and the bone mixture separately. Again cover the bones with cold water, bring to a boil, reduce heat and simmer 4 hours. Periodically skim the foam from the top. Strain, discarding the bones and vegetables. Combine the 2 stocks and reduce by two-thirds.

### FISH STOCK

  5 pounds white fish bones

  2 leeks, sliced

  2 onions, diced

  2 ribs celery, diced

  2 carrots, diced

  2 lemons, halved

  2 bay leaves

  1 tablespoon peppercorns

Place all of the ingredients in a stock pot. Cover with cold water, bring to a boil, reduce the heat and simmer 20 minutes. Strain, discard bones and vegetables, reserve stock.

### VEGETABLE STOCK

  2 yellow onions, diced

  4 ribs celery, diced

  3 carrots, diced

  3 leeks, sliced

  1 tablespoon peppercorns

  2 bay leaves

Place all of the ingredients in a stock pot. Cover with cold water, bring to a boil, reduce heat and simmer 20 minutes. Strain, discard vegetables, reserve stock.

### MUSHROOM STOCK

  2 pounds mushrooms

  2 yellow onions, diced

  3 leeks, sliced

  4 ribs celery, diced

  3 carrots, diced

  1 tablespoon peppercorns

  2 Bay leaves

Place all of the ingredients in a stock pot. Cover with cold water, bring to a boil, reduce heat and simmer 20 minutes. Strain, discard vegetables, reserve stock.

> 1 onion, diced
>
> 2 stalks celery, diced
>
> 2 carrots, peeled and diced
>
> 2 leeks, cleaned and sliced
>
> 10 egg whites
>
> $\frac{1}{2}$ gallon stock
>
> salt and white pepper

Place all of the vegetables in a food processor and pulse until they are very finely diced. Add the egg whites and pulse 2 or 3 times to incorporate. Place the cold stock in a large pot and whisk in the vegetable-egg mixture. Place over medium heat and slowly bring to a simmer. The egg whites will begin to coagulate which will trap all of the impurities in the stock and make it clear. This coagulation will rise to the top. It is called a raft. Punch a hole in the raft and simmer for 1 hour. Place a cheesecloth lined chinois over another pot. Gently move the raft aside and ladle the consommé into the chinois. What you should get is a very clear liquid. Reheat and season with salt and pepper.

## Cooking Lobster and Lobster Stock

It is a disservice to the lobster to plunge it in boiling water and cook it for ten or twelve minutes. It takes 7 years for a lobster to grow to $1\frac{1}{2}$ pounds. If you are going to cook a lobster you should make it the best tasting lobster you can. If you are squeamish about killing the lobster, have them do it before you buy it. If not, follow the directions on page 7. Remove the tail and claws (keeping arm intact) with a twist and pull.

 Bring a small pot of water to a boil. Add the lobster tail, turn off heat and steep 8 minutes. Remove the lobster tail from the pot and shock it in ice water. Bring the water back to a boil, add the claws turn off heat and steep 6 minutes. Remove the claws from the pot and shock them in ice water. Heat 2 tablespoons of oil in another small sauce pot. Add the lobster body and sauté it until it is bright red. Add steeping water, bring to a boil, reduce heat and simmer for 20 minutes. Strain through a chinois and reserve water as lobster stock.

## Sachet d'epices

> 3 parsley stems
>
> 3 thyme sprigs
>
> 2 bay leaves
>
> 5 cracked peppercorns

Place all of the ingredients inside a piece of cheesecloth and tie into a bag with kitchen twine.

## BUTTER, OIL AND CREAM

Three things you need for this book and these recipes. They enhance and enrich flavors and are an excellent medium for cooking, but definitely use them in moderation.

### AÏOLI

> 2 tablespoons minced garlic
>
> 2 egg yolks
>
> 1 teaspoon Dijon mustard
>
> 1 teaspoon fresh lemon juice
>
> 1 cup olive oil
>
> salt and white pepper

Place the garlic, egg yolks, Dijon mustard and lemon juice in the bowl of a food processor. Purée until a pale yellow in color. With the food processor running, slowly add the oil in a thin stream. The aïoli should be the consistency of thin mayonnaise. Season to taste with salt and pepper.

### ROASTED GARLIC AÏOLI

> $1/4$ cup mashed roasted garlic (see method below)
>
> 2 egg yolks
>
> 1 teaspoon Dijon mustard
>
> 1 teaspoon fresh lemon juice
>
> 1 cup roasted garlic oil (see method below)
>
> salt and white pepper

Place the garlic, egg yolks, Dijon mustard and lemon juice in the bowl of a food processor. Purée until a pale yellow in color. With the food processor running, slowly add the roasted garlic oil in a thin stream. The aïoli should be the consistency of thin mayonnaise. Season to taste with salt and pepper.

### ROASTED GARLIC AND ROASTED GARLIC OIL

> 2 heads garlic, peeled
>
> 1 cup olive oil

Preheat the oven to 200°F. Place the garlic cloves and oil in a small oven proof container. Make sure garlic is submerged in oil. Place the garlic in the oven and bake until it is very tender, 45–60 minutes. Cool and strain, reserving the garlic and the oil separately. Mash the garlic cloves into a smooth paste with a fork.

## CLARIFIED BUTTER/ BROWN BUTTER

2 sticks butter

Melt the butter in a small sauce pot. Skim the foam from top. Let the white milk solids settle to the bottom. Pour off the clear golden liquid that is left. That is the clarified butter To make brown butter continue cooking over low heat until butter is brown and smells nutty.

## BEURRE BLANC

3 black peppercorns

1 shallot, peeled and thinly sliced

1 cup white wine

3 tablespoons white wine vinegar

3 tablespoons heavy cream

2 sticks butter, diced

salt and white pepper

1-3 tablespoons fresh lemon juice

Place the peppercorns, shallot, white wine and white wine vinegar in a small saucepot. Place over high heat and reduce until the pan is almost dry. When there is about one tablespoon of liquid left in the pan, add the cream and let that reduce slightly, be careful not to let the cream burn. Reduce the heat to low and start whisking in the butter, one cube at a time until all the butter is incorporated. The sauce should be thick and pale yellow in color. Add salt and pepper to taste. Then add lemon juice to taste, the sauce will thin slightly, but keep it over low heat and it should thicken back up. Strain through chinoise and keep warm until ready to use.

## CRÈME FRAÎCHE

1 cup heavy cream

$\frac{1}{4}$ cup buttermilk

Combine both ingredients in a glass jar with a lid. Place in a warm spot for 24–48 hours until thickened. Stir and then refrigerate for 24 hours.

# OILS

Oils are an integral part of any dish. They add intensity and give each dish that little extra boost of flavor and color. At the restaurant we use a vita-prep blender which eliminates the need to blanch or shock the herbs first.

### TARRAGON OIL
Yield 1 cup

> 3 cups chopped tarragon
>
> 1 cup chopped parsley
>
> 1 cup olive oil

Bring a small pot of water to a boil. Have a small bowl of ice water ready. Place the tarragon and parsley in boiling water for 30 seconds, drain and plunge into the ice bath. Drain. Place the blanched herbs in the blender with the olive oil and purée. Let the mixture rest overnight and then strain through a chinois.

### CHIVE OIL
Yield 1 cup

> 1 cup chopped chives
>
> 2 cups chopped parsley
>
> 1 cup olive oil

Bring a small pot of water to a boil. Have a small bowl of ice water ready. Place the chives and parsley in boiling water for 30 seconds, drain and plunge into ice bath. Drain. Place the blanched herbs in blender with the olive oil and purée. Let the mixture rest overnight and then strain through a chinois.

### BASIL OIL
Yield 1 cup

> 3 cups chopped basil
>
> 1 cup chopped parsley
>
> 1 cup olive oil

Bring a small pot of water to a boil. Have a small bowl of ice water ready. Place the basil and parsley in the boiling water for 30 seconds. Drain and plunge into ice bath. Drain, place the blanched herbs in the blender with the olive oil and purée. Let rest overnight and then strain through a chinois.

## Cilantro Oil
Yield 1 cup

    3 cups chopped cilantro

    1 cup chopped parsley

    1 cup olive oil

Bring a small pot of water to a boil. Have a small bowl of ice water ready. Place the cilantro leaves and parsley in the boiling water for 30 seconds, drain and plunge into the ice bath. Drain. Place the blanched herbs in the blender with the olive oil and purée. Let rest overnight and then strain through a chinois.

## Chili oil
Yield 1 cup

    2 tablespoons chipotle chili in adobo sauce

    3 tablespoons paprika

    1 cup vegetable oil

Place all of the ingredients in a blender and purée. Let sit overnight and then strain.

## Toasted Garlic and Meyer lemon oil
Yield 1 cup

    12 cloves garlic, sliced

    2 Meyer lemons, zested

    1 cup olive oil

Place the garlic, lemon zest and olive oil in a small pot over medium heat. Cook until the garlic is toasted. Let rest overnight and then strain through a chinois.

# DOUGH

## BRIOCHE – 2 LOAVES

> 1 tablespoon active dry yeast
>
> $\frac{1}{3}$ cup milk, scalded and cooled to tepid
>
> 6 eggs, beaten
>
> 4 cups flour
>
> 1 teaspoon salt
>
> 1 tablespoon sugar
>
> $\frac{1}{2}$ pound butter

Mix the yeast, milk, 1 of the eggs and 1 cup of the flour together in the bowl of a standing mixer. Let stand 30 minutes. Add the salt, sugar, and the remaining eggs and flour. Mix on medium speed until the dough is smooth and elastic. Work the butter with a dough scraper until smooth, but still cool. Add the butter a little at a time to the dough with the mixer on low speed. The dough may break apart, but continue mixing, it will come back together. Transfer the dough to a lightly floured surface, knead slightly and place in a buttered bowl. Cover with a towel and let it rise until doubled, $1\frac{1}{2}$–2 hours. Preheat the oven to 325°F and butter your brioche pan. Punch down the dough and divide in half. Roll each half into a rectangle ($9\frac{1}{2}$ x11). The one side of the rectangle should be the same width as your brioche pan. Fold each half of the dough into thirds, (like putting a piece of paper in an envelope), and then roll-up the dough, starting on the layered edge. Seal the ends and place in a the brioche pan, with the seam end at the bottom of the pan. Let rise almost to the top edge of the pan. Bake for 25–35 minutes until a toothpick inserted in the center bottom comes out clean.

## PASTA DOUGH

> 2 cups flour
>
> 1 teaspoon salt
>
> 4 egg yolks
>
> 1 tablespoon olive oil
>
> 2-4 tablespoons water

Place the flour and salt in the bowl of a food processor. Turn the food processor on and add the egg yolks one at a time. Then add the olive oil, and then add enough water to form a smooth elastic dough. Remove the dough from the food processor and wrap in plastic wrap. Let rest for 2 hours in the refrigerator.

## ENGLISH MUFFINS

    1 cup milk

    2 tablespoons butter

    1 tablespoon sugar

    1 teaspoon active dry yeast

    $1\frac{1}{2}$ - 2 cups all purpose flour

    1 cup whole wheat flour

    1 teaspoon salt

    2 tablespoons corn meal

    3 tablespoons olive oil

Heat the milk, butter and sugar until the butter melts and the sugar dissolves. Cool to lukewarm, then add the yeast and let it sit for 5 minutes to activate. Place in the bowl of a standing mixer. Add 1 cup of the all purpose flour, the whole wheat flour and the salt and mix on medium speed for 5 minutes. Add as much remaining all purpose flour as needed to form a smooth dough. Remove the dough from the mixer and knead an additional 5 minutes. Place the dough in a buttered bowl and let rise until double ($1\frac{1}{2}$–2 hours). Punch down, let rest 5 minutes then roll out to $\frac{1}{2}$ inch thickness. Cut out muffins with a 3 inch ring mold, and press each side into the cornmeal. Brush oil on a flat grill on medium high heat. Place the muffins on the grill and cook for about 30 minutes, turning the muffins often to avoid burning. You may need to turn the heat down to medium. When ready to serve, slice the muffins in half and toast lightly, then spread with butter.

## MISCELLANEOUS

### ROASTING PEPPERS

    2 red peppers

    2 tablespoons olive oil

Preheat the oven to 400°F or turn on the grill. Coat the peppers with the oil. Place them on a baking sheet in the oven or on a grill. Roast until the peppers are blackened on all sides. Place the peppers in a bag to steam until they are cool. Remove the blackened skins and the seeds.

### BOUQUET GARNI

    1 stalk celery

    $\frac{1}{2}$ leek

    3 or 4 parsley stems

    2 sprigs fresh thyme

    1 fresh bay leaf

Cut the celery stalk in half and place leek, parsley, thyme and bay leaf between the 2 pieces of celery. Tie together with kitchen twine.

### TOASTED PINE NUTS, WALNUTS, HAZELNUTS, ALMONDS

Place the nuts in a sauté pan large enough to hold them in an even layer. Place the sauté pan over low heat for 10–15 minutes until the nuts are fragrant.

### POWDERS

Be creative. These are a few suggestions of ingredients to use, do each one seperately!

    1 red onion, diced

    1 yellow onion, diced

    1 red beet, diced

    1 cup peas

    3 cups basil leaves

    1 red pepper, seeded and diced

Preheat oven to 200°F. Lay the ingredients on a baking sheet in an even layer. Leave in oven until fully dried, 2-6 hours depending on the ingredient. Pulverize in a spice grinder. These will keep for an extended period of time in air tight container.

# COOKING EQUIPMENT AND TERMS

**Acidulated water** To add an acid, like lemon juice, lime juice or vinegar, to water to soak fruits or vegetables that are likely to brown when exposed to air.

**Batonnet** To cut into uniform size rectangles.

**Brunoise** To uniformly cut into very small squares.

**Chiffonade** To lay lettuce leaves or herbs on top of one another and roll them together into a cylinder, then finely slice to get uniform strips.

**Chinoise** A very fine mesh conical sieve used to strain sauces, soups and purées.

**Coulis** To pureé a fruit, vegetable or herb into a small concentrated sauce.

**Deglaze** To remove browned bits from the bottom of a hot pan that has been used to sear meat by adding wine or stock.

**Dice** To uniformily cut into squares.

**Julienne** To slice into long thin uniform strips.

**Mandoline** A hand operated slicer that can be adjusted to make uniform cuts of varying thickness.

**Mince** To very finely chop.

**Quenelle** Using two spoons to shape a soft, but stable food like mashed potates into a 3 sided oval.

**Resting** To remove cooked meat from heat and cover with foil for 10 minutes before cutting. This is very important to let the meat relax and the juices redistribute throughout.

**Rice** To press cooked potatoes through a kitchen utensil called a ricer. Which looks like a large garlic press, the potato is forced through small holes to make it look like rice.

**Ring Molds** A circular shaped cookie cutter made of aluminum and can range in diameter from 1–7 inches.

**Sachet d'epices** To place a mixture of herbs in a piece of cheesecloth and tie into a bag then add to soups, stocks or sauces for flavoring. It usually includes bay leaves, peppercorns, parsley stems, and thyme sprigs.

**Sauté** To cook over high heat in a small amount of oil for a short period of time.

**Sweat** To cook over low heat in a covered pot in a little fat to avoid coloring.

**Tamis** A flat fine mesh sieve used to strain soups, sauces and purées.

**Truffle slicer** A special tool used to slice truffles paper thin.

**Trussed** To tie with kitchen twine into a compact shape.

**Vitaprep blender** A patented high power blender.